I HOPE YOU'RE HAPPY

Stories

MARNI APPLETON

THE
INDIGO
PRESS

For my sisters

THE INDIGO PRESS
50 Albemarle Street
London W1S 4BD
www.theindigopress.com

The Indigo Press Publishing Limited Reg. No. 10995574
Registered Office: Wellesley House, Duke of Wellington Avenue
Royal Arsenal, London SE18 6SS

Cover design © Luke Bird
Cover photograph © French Anderson Ltd
Art direction by House of Thought
Typeset by Tetragon, London
Printed and bound in Great Britain by CPI Group (UK) Ltd, Croydon CR0 4YY

CONTENTS

Say the ape, the Eurasian magpie, or the elephant looks in the mirror and recognizes the paint smeared on her body by the researcher. The animal who passes the mirror test then investigates her own body for the offending mark. Say she finds nothing. How long before she trusts the reflection over her own body? Say the mark on her reflection is confirmed by all the other elephants. How long before her reflection replaces herself?

Melissa Febos, *Girlhood*

Give me back my girlhood, it was mine first.

Taylor Swift

Shut Your Mouth

00.03. Tuesday night. A hazy shape, static against the darkness. Ponytail, puffa jacket, handbag. A girl, like a blast of light.

The CCTV footage slows as the girl leaves the fried chicken shop. A box of food clutched to her chest with one hand, phone in the other. She taps on the screen as she walks down the road and slips out of shot – a moment of lunar emptiness, a bright crackle – before the door swings open and she steps out into the street again. The clip loops on repeat. I scour the screen, looking for something: a tiny detail, an overlooked speck of evidence, eyes glinting from the bushes. There must be something we are not seeing.

I return to the search page and click onto a message board for amateur sleuths. It is full of non-professionals who are, like me, trying to cobble together pieces of evidence to create a fuller picture. I learn that her last text was sent at 00.11. GPS records show that at this point she was on her usual route home, approximately five minutes' walk from her flat. Two minutes later, her phone was turned off (or destroyed). It has not yet been switched back on. At the bottom of the page, the comments: *She can't have just disappeared. She can't have vanished into thin air.*

Kirsten sweeps into my room without knocking. I snap the laptop shut. Daylight seeps from the sky, the colour of dirty dishwater. She switches on the main light, a bare bulb. It makes my eyes ache.

You're not even dressed yet.

I'm not going.

You'll like it when we get there.

I don't want to.

It'll be fun.

I flop back onto my bed in protest and turn my head towards Kirsten, now double Kirsten: one Kirsten looking at the other in my full-length mirror. She's wearing a dress I haven't seen before. It looks new. Black halter, sweetheart neckline and a tucked waist, printed all over with blood-red cherries.

Wasn't that style popular like, a hundred years ago? Don't you think it's kind of dated?

No, Kirsten says to herself in the mirror. It's right on the pulse. She turns this way and that, swishes her skirt. Cherries dance across the glass.

Kirsten and I know each other from school. We weren't close then; not like we are now. We moved out of halls and in with each other last year. Technically, we also live with a woman named Sandra – she owns the house and pays the council tax – but she's always away on business. We see her sporadically, maybe twice a month. Her suits are always crisp, clean and crease-free, even when she claims to have been travelling all day. When she's gone, Sandra keeps her bedroom door locked. The house is blank and pristine, like a hotel or an Airbnb. She never leaves any personal items out, nothing to betray her interests or taste. Kirsten and I navigate the shared spaces carefully, as though we are visiting. We never invite our friends over. Most evenings, we huddle up on Sandra's slate-grey corner sofa and watch sitcoms on Netflix. But at least once a week Kirsten insists that we go 'out out'.

I drag myself up from the bed. I put on a clinging velvet dress, midnight blue, black tights, boots. I barely glance at myself in the mirror. Kirsten rakes some product through my hair and scrunches it at the ends. I whine all the way down the road that my feet hurt, then stare out of the bus window while she sends a stream of WhatsApps confirming that we are indeed on our way. When we get to the bar, everyone is talking about some photo.

Have you seen it?

You haven't?

Best photo of the year, hands down.

The label of my beer has become soggy with condensation. It peels off in long, satisfying strips. Kirsten glares at me. I never try with these things. We stand at the edge of a cluster of people. Kirsten: smiling, engaging, trying to work her way in. Me: staring into my bottle and wondering when our peers became so well versed in photography that they were qualified to diagnose the single best photograph of the entire year.

I just think it's really sexy, says this guy, Luke, a second year, whose blonde fringe is parted at the centre of his forehead. Does everything have to be a political statement? Can't we move past all that and share in the experience of a beautiful woman enjoying herself?

I completely agree, Shell chips in. That's what's so empowering about it. The freedom, the pleasure. It's sad that a woman enjoying food is something that has to be commented on. Isn't it time we talked about something else?

An image comes into my mind: the missing woman, the fried chicken, her lips and fingers slick with grease. Kirsten nods and nods like her head is malfunctioning.

Like, haven't we moved on since the noughties? says Luke. You know, Kate Moss, Amy Winehouse. Heroin chic or whatever. That was such a sad time.

Luke gazes past us; a reverent hush settles over the group. I make a face at Kirsten, but she is staring at him with wide, shining eyes, like he's something she could eat.

I go to the toilet to be on my own. The plastic lid creaks under my weight. I search on my phone for the famous photo, tap with my fingertip, and the thumbnail swells to full size. A young woman tucked into a white plastic garden chair, her pale knees bumping against each other, white-socked ankles crossed. The grass shimmers in the background, a false, supersaturated green, like something from Dr Seuss. After a beat, I recognize the woman, a famous supermodel. I've never seen her like this: relaxed, dressed down, casual. She is blurred somehow, ever so slightly out of focus. The real subject of the photo isn't her at all, but the hot dog, which she holds out in two hands, ketchup dripping between her long fingers. The red sauce is lurid and other-worldly, stark against the grass, like something pretending to be natural; fake blood or lipstick. The inside of the sausage glistens pinkly in the sunshine. But the photo isn't the way you might imagine, grotesque and vulgar – in fact, it *is* an interesting image. Tasteful even. The woman's mouth is full: a bulge in the soft meat of her cheek, her head turned slightly from the camera. Within hours of being posted, it had garnered more likes than Ariana Grande's wedding pictures, enough to rival the Instagram egg.

In bed that night, I open the image on my phone again. I trace the outline of the woman's face, the smooth curve of the hot dog. I swipe from the photo to the news. The missing woman has slipped down a few tiers on the site, become a little less newsworthy. The hot dog is ahead of her: FLUKE 'AESTHETICALLY PERFECT' PHOTOGRAPH ON TRACK TO RECEIVE THE MOST INSTAGRAM LIKES IN HISTORY. I look at it for a long time. After a while, my mouth waters. I realize I am hungry.

The next day, I decide to visit the chicken shop. I want to get down there, into the thick of the investigation. It's not that I necessarily think I'll find the girl – that would be ridiculous – but I have a strong feeling there's a connection between us. Perhaps I could be useful. On the bus, I scroll through the news. There are no updates. The police are keen to emphasize that this remains a missing person case, not a murder investigation. I told Kirsten I wasn't well to explain why I was skipping uni. She sends me a text to ask how I'm feeling. I reply with a sad face emoji, which is not a complete lie. The hot dog photo is everywhere on my social feeds. Vegans and animal rights activists have spoken out about the fact that it 'glorifies the consumption of meat'. Health campaigners aren't impressed either, claiming that public figures have a responsibility to encourage healthy eating. Kirsten sends me a hug emoji, then she sends me an opinion piece with the headline THE IMAGE THAT SINGLE-HANDEDLY ELIMINATED FOOD-BASED SHAME.

People are losing their minds, Kirsten writes. *They need to get a grip.*

I thought you liked it? I text back.

It's not about liking it. It's about being realistic about its impact.

I get off the bus on Roderham Road. It's a wide street, residential. The houses are mostly Victorian terraces with brightly coloured front doors and brass knockers. The chicken shop is further down, between a newsagent and a beauty salon. What happened here? I whisper to myself, like I am narrating a documentary. I turn on my phone's camera and film the journey up the road. I will analyse the footage later.

The chicken shop is busy for a Thursday morning. It's only 10 a.m. and not long opened. Red plastic chairs, screwed to the ground. Yellow tabletops. Colours that make me think of preschool. When I get to the front of the queue, I ask the guy behind the till if he knows what the missing girl ordered. He frowns and looks down at his blue-gloved hands. His cap covers his face so I can't read his expression.

I'm not supposed to talk about that any more, he says, head still bowed.

I am aware of the people behind me, impatient, ravenous. That's okay, I say, leaning forward. I'm not press or anything. Just curious.

He looks up at me then, looks me right in the eye. So, you want a three-piece chicken meal with regular fries and a strawberry Mirinda?

Yes. I nod slowly, knowingly. Yes, that's what I want.

I had hoped there would be more clues in her choice of meal. For example, there would be lots to read into the choice to order twenty extra-hot wings. Or perhaps she would have ordered enough food for four people, and then I could try to work out who she was going to see. But no. Her order was nothing special. It was what I usually ordered after a night out. It was what anyone would order.

So, I say, fishing in my purse for cash. Have you been busier since... you know?

Yes. It's been busy, very busy. Nearly back to normal now though. That'll be £5.99. He takes the cash and his eyes slide over me and onto the person behind. Next, please.

There aren't any seats free, but that's fine. I had always planned to walk out of here with my food. I put my can of Mirinda in my bag, and I think: she must have put her can of Mirinda in her bag. I clutch the box of chicken to my chest, hold my phone in my other hand. The door swings shut behind me. I turn right and start walking down the road.

I take out my phone again to film the route, turning it this way and that to capture all the houses, anywhere she could have turned off, the food cooling against my body. Halfway down the road, I come across the entrance to a patch of woodland. I've seen it before, on Google Maps, a cluster of broccoli among the miniature houses. It is cordoned off now, with white-and-blue police tape. I tell myself to cross the road, duck under the tape and look around, but I can't. I want to find clues; I want to find her alive. I don't want to find her dead body. I stand there for another minute, willing myself into action, still filming. Then I turn and head back towards the bus stop. I start eating the chips. They're cold and soggy, but I didn't eat breakfast.

Kirsten is in the kitchen when I get home, slicing up hot dogs to put on top of her salad.

Where have you been?

I take off my jacket and slide onto one of the bar stools.

Out.

Out where? You're supposed to be sick.

I felt better.

She sits down opposite me and starts to eat her lunch. I watch her chew iceberg lettuce and frankfurter, flashes of green and fleshy pink appearing and disappearing as she moves her mouth, like clothes in a washing machine.

You smell disgusting, Kirsten says.

Thank you.

I mean it. You smell like grease.

Interesting.

You went to the chicken shop, didn't you?

I shrug.

You've got to stop with this obsession! It's unhealthy. What exactly were you hoping to find? Blood on the pavement? Her bag in a nearby dustbin? I can't believe you.

But –

Please, just stop. Like, it's time to move on?

I look at the granite worktop, its flashes of light like stars in the night sky. I realize I don't know what I was hoping to find. I wanted to be there, to do something.

The police must know something you don't, Kirsten says, as though she's read my mind. Maybe she's run away or killed herself or something.

I nod, like these would be reassuring outcomes.

At the weekend, my mum visits. We get lunch at a fancy place in town. We sit at a table by the window so we can watch the Saturday shoppers moving past in a continuous stream, like brightly coloured fish in an aquarium. My mum orders a tomato and burrata salad with balsamic vinegar. I choose white fish in a creamy sauce with garlic buttered potatoes. She's on her own. My dad is in Taiwan on a work trip.

He wanted to come, Mum says, her voice syrupy and sorry.

Afterwards, we walk around the busy shopping centre together. We look at lots of clothes – it gives us something to talk about – but we never try anything on. Eventually, we go into Boots. My mum buys me some new deodorant and moisturizer, a jumbo pack of maxi pads. We try out a few of the perfumes. One in particular catches my eye. It's called Savoureux, which the salesgirl tells us means 'tasty' in French. Behind her, an enormous poster of a woman with dark, hollowed-out eyes, hunched over a plate of ribs, up to her elbows in sauce. It smells like caramel and metal. My mum buys it for me as a gift.

Lying in bed that evening, I read an article about this year's unlikeliest fashion trend: food. There are photos of an actress who wore a dress made of pasta to the Met Gala, headpieces made from hollowed-out watermelon bowls on the runway at Dolce & Gabbana. The Savoureux ad is featured, as well as a skincare campaign with dozens of girls lying on a pink satin-covered bed, eating pizza. I look at them, stretched out and effortlessly beautiful, surrounded by pillows. Their skin is perfect. Mouths open, catlike. Tongues waiting to catch globs of melted cheese.

Kirsten appears in my doorway. Look at this, she says, looming over me.

I shut my laptop and replace it with hers. On the screen, a photo of Kirsten, riding the Tube and eating a doughnut. Her mouth is open; she is poised, ready to take another bite. There are flecks of icing and sprinkles on her skirt and dusting her upper lip.

What do you think?

Um, I say. Who took it?

There isn't anything especially artistic about the photo. It's blurry and taken at a somewhat unflattering angle,

Kirsten's eyes half-closed as though they're rolling back in her head.

I don't know. Does it matter?

What do you mean you don't know?

It's on this new group... But that's not the point. Do you *like* it?

What group?

Okay, okay, she says, shuffling me along to make space for herself on my mattress. Someone started this group online. At first it was called something like *Women Eating on the Underground*, because it started in London, but now it's got pictures of women from all over the world. You're not allowed to post photos of yourself or people you know, only strangers. Look...

She clicks through to the main page and scrolls. She shows me a photo: an older woman sits on a bench, hair tied in a scarf, mouth closing on a sandwich.

This one's from Lyon, Kirsten says, and this one... This one's New York. She expands a photo of a pre-teen girl on a subway platform. She is wearing rainbow tie-dye shorts and eating a pastry. And who knows where this one is, she says, opening a video of a woman eating a chicken dish in the economy section of a plane. Somewhere above us, right now, there's a woman eating... It's brilliant!

I watch the woman on the plane over and over again. The way her eyes dart around as though she knows she is being watched. The way she chews quickly and swallows hard, her forehead centimetres from the seat in front. She dabs her lips with a napkin after every forkful.

And now there's a photo of me in the group too, Kirsten says, with satisfaction.

And you're happy about that?

Kirsten surveys my face. I thought you'd be pleased for me. I didn't think you would be jealous.

I snort. I'm not jealous.

Yeah… Okay, you're not jealous.

I'm not. I think you're being stupid.

Stupid?

It's creepy, Ki. It's an invasion of your privacy.

Wow. Thanks for your concern.

Kirsten leaves my room and slams the door behind her. The framed postcards on my wall shudder. I open the group page on my phone and swipe through endless – literally endless – photographs of women eating. I wonder how long Kirsten had been looking before she saw herself materialize on the page like a mirage, like a gift. There is a picture I recognize, of a woman biting into a muffin. I don't know the woman, but she has been turned into a meme, variations on a theme. You know: *Get a girl who looks at you the way this woman looks at this muffin.* Some images I scroll past, but others make me stop. The woman in a car, eating fast food from a paper bag, fries dangling from her mouth, gaze fixed on the road ahead. The woman on a bench in the spring sunshine, eating an ice cream. Eyes closed, a moment of perfect contentment.

I wait for some sort of feminist backlash, but it doesn't come. Everyone seems to find the group amusing and unproblematic, which makes me wonder if I might be jealous after all. I don't know what else to call the tangle of anger and uneasiness in the pit of my belly, and that seems as good a name as any. I look carefully through the photos on the group. It's true that they all seem to be posted in a festive, celebratory spirit. And there is something powerful about it, the intensity with which these women are desired, and desire. I read the comments on each photo. They say things like *I like a woman with a big appetite* or *I wish my wife ate like this* or *We love to see it!!* Sometimes women comment on each other's photos, in a supportive, sisterly way: *Bite of dreams* or *Perfect chew, hun.*

After that, I stop eating in public. It feels like the virtuous thing to do. But sometimes I crack open a packet of crisps at the bus stop to feel a frisson of danger. The packet puffs and crackles and the air turns solid. Nobody moves. What would happen if I took a crisp out of the packet and put it in my mouth? What if I crunched it with my teeth, chewed and swallowed? Would people watch me, take photos? Would somebody hurt me, maybe even kill me? Eventually, I put the crisps back inside my bag, open and uneaten, beside the can of Mirinda. The air changes. The other people at the stop let out their breath collectively; disappointed perhaps, or relieved. I touch the can of Mirinda, dented and garishly pink. It has become a kind of talisman. I tell myself I'll open it when the missing girl is found.

The weather brightens. Blossom bursts into life and the daffodils go crispy at the frills, as though nature itself is frazzled by the sudden seasonal shift. More girls go missing. The influencer who was last seen by the delivery guy who dropped off her Chinese takeaway. The middle-aged mum who was last seen collecting a cake for her daughter's birthday. I watch the video of her buckling the cake box into the front seat over and over until my vision blurs. My books are stacked on my desk, but I can't bring myself to open them. The words swim away from me when I try. What little energy I have leaches slowly from my body and into my phone. I am tense and jittery without it, can only breathe when I am watching something: a police press conference or a video of a cat or a baby or both, celebrities strolling around their extravagant houses answering seventy-three random questions. I learn whether they prefer tea or coffee, city or beach, burgers or pasta.

I am lying on the grass on the quad, my back slightly damp, when I spot Kirsten and Shell walking towards me. I lower my sunglasses and wave. There is something different about them.

What have you got on your faces?

What d'you mean? says Shell, her voice muffled by the shimmery material strung over her mouth.

What do you mean, what do I mean?

Huh?

I turn to Kirsten, who is taking a pair of sunglasses out of her bag. She shrugs. It's just a voile, she says.

I continue to stare.

It's this face accessory so you can't see our mouths properly, not in detail anyway.

I don't get it. Why are you hiding your mouth?

I'm not. I love my mouth. It's... Well... Don't you ever feel exposed? When you walk around with your mouth just... out like that?

Yeah, says Shell. When you think about it, it's kind of gross.

I bring my hand to my face instinctively and finger my lips. Supple and soft, different to the other types of skin I have on show. I breathe out of my mouth sometimes. It is an opening, a hole that leads to my tongue, my throat, my insides. All slick membranes and private flesh. Kirsten and Shell are right: it feels weird that it is out, on display, for anyone to look at.

Sandra is home that night. Kirsten and I open the door to see her heels placed neatly together on the shoe rack, a suitcase waiting on the freshly vacuumed carpet.

Girls! Sandra calls to us from the kitchen. Hello there. It's only a flying one. Back out on the road tomorrow.

We become children again in her presence. We smile and mumble. I think about how I watched a TikTok of someone describing this as 'smumbling'. Why is it that the smart girls are always smumbling? they said. Speak up, ladies! We want to hear your voices!

Would you like a glass of wine?

Sandra is already halfway through a bottle of red most definitely not bought from a supermarket. Kirsten and I look at each other.

Sure, Kirsten says. Thank you.

Sandra looks at me and raises her eyebrows. I nod.

So, Sandra says. How's it all going? How's university life? How's the house? No problems, I trust.

Kirsten and I glance at each other again. This is unlike Sandra. Usually she greets us cursorily, without questions or interest. We see her eating something in the kitchen – a salad if it's dinner time or a bowl of muesli first thing in the morning – then she's gone again, or shut away in her room, preparing to creep away at the crack of dawn.

Oh yeah, Kirsten says. It's all going well, thank you. And of course we love the house.

Yes, we love the house, I say.

Fantastic. Sandra smiles and pours herself another glass of wine. I can hear the tick of the clock, the gentle hiss of the dishwasher.

This is great wine, says Kirsten. Thank you, Sandra.

Look, girls, Sandra says, cutting her off, suddenly serious. I need to talk to you about something. It's nothing to worry about, not for you anyway, but... ah. Well, I'll not beat about the bush. There are some... photographs of my friends and me doing the rounds on the internet. You might not have seen them yet, but I expect you will. It's all a rather unfortunate breach of our privacy, you see. We're incredibly upset about it, and we're taking the necessary steps to have these images removed. But in the meantime, well... They're out there. And it seems there's nothing we can do about it.

Oh, Kirsten says. Gosh.

I don't say any actual words, but I nod and make sounds, not trusting myself to speak.

Oh goodness, Sandra says. I've worried you both. I can see it in your eyes. I'm fine! We're all fine. It's just one of those internet things, isn't it? You never know when it'll be your turn in the spotlight. And – oh! Oh dear. I haven't led you to think these images are in any way *sexual*, have I? No, no. Of course, it's nothing like that. We were just... well. We were in a restaurant. We were eating. We were in a private dining room, or at least it was supposed to be a private dining room. It was my friend's birthday...

Sandra reaches for her wine glass, and I notice that her hand is trembling.

We google the images together later, huddled up in Kirsten's bed. They have been posted in the *Women Eating...* group. In fact, they are currently the top-viewed photos. In the first photos, the six women are perfectly composed: cheeks powdered, clothes pressed, hair coiffed. They lean towards each other for dainty air kisses, like flowers swaying on a stem. Then they begin to eat. They slurp oysters from their shells, crack langoustines with their bare hands and suck the juice from their heads. They crunch on deep-fried baby squid and swipe slices of sourdough through mounds of mackerel pâté. By the end of the meal, the women are glassy-eyed and glossy-lipped, dishevelled and satisfied. The last photo depicts two of the women: one stretching her legs out, feet resting in the lap of the other. The slanted afternoon light falls across their faces, washing them in pink, giving the photo a dreamlike quality. We almost don't recognize Sandra, a dab of sauce on her chin, her head thrown back in laughter. Another woman clasps a glass of wine and gazes tenderly in her direction.

Sandra, eh? Kirsten says. Who knew?

Shh! She might hear you.

We read on. That morning, the women had released a joint statement, calling for an investigation into who took the photographs and 'disseminated them without consent'. They used words like 'outrage', 'violation' and 'illegal'. They wanted the person who 'stole' their images to be brought to justice. They called for the 'grossly misogynistic' group to be shut down. They called for the restaurant itself to be shut down. They called for prison time. They called for the government to investigate the public safety standards the restaurant had breached.

This is a bit much, isn't it? says Kirsten. They're only photos.

I didn't realize it was a crime to take photos of people.

Sounds like they're making a lot of fuss over nothing.

We return to the photos. They are magnificent photos. They stir something in me, a ripple spreading out from my navel to the ends of my hair. I feel alive, like when I stand at the top of a tall building, or in front of a great work of art, as though all the world is collapsing into this one, singular moment. There is something warming about these photos: the women's visible satisfaction, their glistening mouths.

I guess they didn't exactly volunteer themselves for this, I say. I mean, they were just eating.

But they were eating in a public place. No one is being

nasty about them – all the comments are positive! Or…
they were…

Kirsten stops at a recent comment and we both flinch.

Bloody hell, I say.

Well, Kirsten says. People are upset, aren't they? They
were getting good attention, the right kind of attention.
They should have enjoyed their time in the spotlight.

I wrap a pair of tights over my face to go to the shop. It
is the kind of place that sells all sorts of accessories, from
handbags to socks, phone cases, lip balm, sunglasses. I knew
they'd sell voiles. They have a whole wall full of them,
in many different colours, patterns and styles. You could
choose a different one to go with every outfit. At the till,
the saleswoman tries to tempt me with a new product, a
kind of glue that keeps your lips stuck together for a few
hours. It means you can show off your lips in a risqué way
but still keep it classy, she explains. You know, when you
want to be that extra bit sexy for a date night or something
but don't want to leave yourself exposed. No slips! She
smiles beneath her own lilac silk voile.

The choice is overwhelming. I walk around the shop a
few times, peering at everything on sale. In the end, I stick
with the one voile, the first one I'd seen. It is kind of plain –
black lace – but I figure I can wear it with a few different
outfits.

Great choice! says the saleswoman as she scans my voile,
bags it up and asks me to tap my card. Next time, look
out for our silk and satin range, she adds. They're sold out

today, but we're due a delivery next week. They're so good for your skin!

I nod and smile broadly as I back out of the shop. Then I clasp a hand over my mouth.

When I get home, I tell Kirsten about the glue.

Don't you think it's weird though? Literally gluing your mouth shut?

Kirsten is applying peach pink lip gloss and looking at herself in the mirror. That depends on what's more important to you, doesn't it? she says, carefully lowering her voile. Looking elegant and in control... or being able to speak.

I know which one is more important to you!

She shrugs. Women have died for my right to speak, she says.

Is that even true?

I'm pretty sure. Are you going to wear your voile tonight? Let's see it on.

I wear red lipstick underneath the voile. At first I'm not sure it's worth it, but it makes me feel better. Knowing it is there makes me feel powerful, even if no one can see it. I match it with a sheer blouse, a black lacy bra and a pair of black leather trousers. Then I spritz myself with Savoureux.

You look badass, Kirsten says, nodding approvingly. Like Catwoman or something.

I scowl, but I am secretly pleased.

Kirsten is lounging on the carpet, wearing nothing but a voile and her underwear. Her phone pings: she turns it over. Oh my god, she says. Have you seen this?

I try to read over her shoulder, but she is scrolling too fast.

It's Sandra and the women from that restaurant.

What about them?

They've given another statement. In person this time. They're actually taking the restaurant to court. Kirsten snorts. This is gonna be a bloodbath.

She angles her phone towards me, and I look at the photograph of the women standing together with their lawyer. They look older and colder, their faces drawn tight shut, impenetrable. It's supposed to be a defiant photo. A display of their strength and solidarity. But all I can think is how lost they look, how tired. Stripped of everything that made the photos special. It could have been easy for them if only they hadn't kicked up such a fuss.

Kirsten wriggles into her new jumpsuit. It's white, tightly fitted, with wide legs and bell sleeves. A showstopper.

Wow, I say. You look insane.

I know, right, she says. Let's take a selfie.

Kirsten posts the photo on Instagram. We look great together, her shimmery blue voile and my black lace. She's right: I do look badass. I watch the likes stack up.

Hey, can I have this?

I turn around. Kirsten is holding the scratched-up can of Mirinda. It must have rolled out of my bag.

Please? I have a little vodka left, but no mixer. Well, except for squash. But it's horrible with squash.

Pressure builds in my chest. I am holding my breath. It's the missing girl's drink, I think. But of course it isn't.

It's just a drink I bought weeks ago that I've been carrying around with me ever since.

Hello? Kirsten says, waving the can through the air.

Uh, sure, I say. No problem.

She pops the tab. It sounds like a bone snapping. Bubbles rush to the surface. For a split second I worry that it's going to explode, that she's going to spill it all over her brand-new outfit.

Do you want some? Kirsten takes a sip, then she proffers her glass. It's not too strong.

I lift the glass to my lips, taste the sugary synthetic fizz on my tongue. I am still waiting for something, some kind of magical retribution. But nothing happens, nothing at all.

I pass the glass back to Kirsten and she drains the rest in one gulp. All right, she says. Ready to go?

We check ourselves out in the hallway mirror. She tweaks my hair, and I tweak it back again. We adjust our voiles, smile at our reflections, and we head out. Into the night.

Under the
Circumstances

Sweet air, divine light! How long have we waited for this
happy sight? This ancient city, its sun-baked streets, the
Acropolis in the distance, raging with light. We are here,
so it begins.

The first night. Everybody orders wine. It comes in little
jugs called carafes. Red or white, it doesn't matter. We simply
ask for krasí, and later ouzo. We say parakaló too, when we
remember. The bartender tells us we shouldn't do shots.
Ouzo is to sip slowly, he tells us. We nod, but when he turns
his back, we down it anyway. The drink is cloudy-white and
smells medicinal. Sophie holds off the longest, sniffing her
glass suspiciously for several minutes. When she finally takes
a sip, she screws up her face and gasps. We cheer. The boys
laugh. The bartender rolls his eyes and mutters something to
a customer. We know we are being ridiculous, but we don't
care. We are here, finally, and everything is as we imagined.
We smoke cheap cigarettes from crushed packets. We try
shisha. We hear the summer breeze shushing through the

cypress boughs, the crackle of ancient history alive in the air. The boys tell us the ouzo will crystallize in our stomachs and that when we drink water in the morning we will become drunk again. This seems entirely possible. Everything seems possible. We could turn objects to gold with one touch, flap our way into the sky, towards the brightness of the sun. Around 1 a.m., the teachers urge us back to the hotel and we go, stumbling, laughing – about what, who knows, who can remember? One of the teachers says the first night is always a bit bacchanalian. We laugh at his choice of word; we get the reference.

All hail Dionysus! we shout.

We should make a sacrifice, Nico says.

I'll kill your firstborn daughter, Leo calls back.

We erupt.

When we get back to the hotel, some of us head to the bar, but the vibe is not what we had hoped for: tinkling piano music, low lighting. The drinks are expensive. The single, besuited bartender regards us without a smile. Our enthusiasm wanes. We head upstairs. Some of us stumble to bed, while others continue drinking from bottles of wine stashed at the backs of wardrobes, under beds.

All hail Dionysus! Anwar shouts, alone, on the stairs.

No one responds. The silence tells him it's time to go to bed.

We wake early the next morning, the sun poking its insistent fingers through the cracks in the hotel curtains. We have so much to do, so much to see! The teachers tell us the schedule earnestly – No dilly-dallying please, we've got a very busy day! We have studied hard, written essays, debated, taken exams, and now, finally, this is our reward. We will walk in the footsteps of Plato, Aristotle, Socrates, in the shadow of the Olympian gods.

But first, Nico tells us about how he vomited in the shower. It was properly projectile, he says. Like a fountain.

Gross, says Katy.

I feel fine now though, Nico says. And I drank almost a litre of water this morning and haven't got drunk again, so thank god for that.

The ouzo is just dissolving. You'll be sloshed in half an hour, says Anwar.

I've got a headache, Leo whines. I need a paracetamol.

Sophie rubs his back. You boys! You never know when to stop.

We chatter as we load up our plates at the buffet: yoghurts, sweet pastries, olives, bread, cheese, boiled eggs cut in half like happy yellow suns. The floor-to-ceiling windows are thrown open to the bright morning. A soundtrack of city sounds, beeping horns and busy breakfast clatter. The stories keep coming. Who else was sick? Who passed out? Who fell over on their way back to the hotel? One of our group is missing – Molly. She tiptoed into our room, quietly quietly, as the day was breaking, the stars shrunk, the night almost nothing, hair matted around her face. Where is she now? When we all left for breakfast, she was still in the shower, washing herself over and over. Maybe she's sick. Maybe she's still drunk.

Downstairs, in the hustle and bustle of the restaurant, we are having fun. We forget Molly. Wait, who danced in the street? Who said what to which teacher? We laugh and laugh and laugh.

On the third day we leave Athens, sunburned and exhausted, to board the cruise ship. It is another glorious day, the sea smooth and shiny like crushed silk. Our ship is called *Antigone*. We are disappointed; we haven't learned the tragedies yet. Our set text for this year is *The Odyssey*. We would have preferred to board the other ship in the cruise company's fleet, *Scylla*, but that ship sails in the wrong direction, west around the jagged coast of mainland Greece and on towards Italy. We love the tale of Scylla, the beautiful nymph turned man-eating monster, and Circe, the witch-goddess who transformed her enemies into pigs.

There is a photo of us lined up in front of the cruise ship, the only photo Molly is in. A row of girls, all smiles. The luminous colours of clothes that have not yet been washed, the false shop sheen shimmering in the sun. One of the teachers counted us down: three, two, one, smile! We all smiled. Molly did too, wide-lipped, full of teeth. Later, we looked at that smile and asked: how could she? How could she smile, after what she'd done? Back then we thought nothing of it, the way she did as she was told and floated along with us throughout the day, like debris on the surface of the sea. Later we cropped her out so only her arm remained, strung up in thin air like a dead thing.

In the room, the narrow room with three sets of bunk beds and not enough space to move, we ask Molly if she is all right. She says she is fine, just tired. She doesn't unpack her bag. She leaves it on the neatly made bed and goes for a walk alone on the deck, her hair whipping her face in the wind. She looks out to sea, the great expanse of water that now lies between us and the mainland, a million miles away.

At dinner, we sit at a round table. Pressed white tablecloth, moussaka. A terrible combination. Halfway through the meal, Leo sidles up, wanting to talk to Sophie. In private. She smiles and excuses herself. On the other side of the table, Molly drops her cutlery and pushes her chair back with a screech. Her food, barely touched, abandoned. Are you all right/what's wrong/everything okay? we ask, words overlapping. She's been acting strange all day. We call to her – Molly! – but she doesn't look back. She rushes out of the door like she's going to be sick. We try to decide who should go after her, but then we notice Katy's face has turned white. Her eyes are wet and terrified.

Katy? What's going on? What do you know?

Just then, Sophie's voice cuts through the din: What the fuck?

Katy bursts into tears. We rush to Sophie's side. We forget about Molly. She's gone, disappeared into the bowels of the ship. We follow Sophie back to our room, our arms around her as though we could physically protect her from what has already been done. We collapse onto the bottom bunks, crammed in together, a tangle of bare limbs.

Get that bag out of here now, Sophie commands.

We chuck Molly's things into the corridor; we'll deal with them later.

Sophie speaks first, telling us what she knows, then Katy fills in the gaps, in sodden, tremulous whispers.

Molly told Katy after we boarded the ship, the two of them alone in the toilets. She locked the door and said: Can I tell you something? Katy is a kind person. Of course she said yes. She didn't know what was going to come next. How could she? Molly held on to Katy's hand and asked what she should do. We didn't ask Katy what advice she gave, why she didn't snatch her hand away. It didn't seem fair. She was put in a difficult position, an impossible position, by Molly. Who of us could say with confidence that we would have done the right thing, caught off guard like that? Still, when Katy tells Sophie that she knew, hours before the rest of us, she hangs her head in shame, shrinks up inside herself like a deflated balloon. Sophie listens to her, and we sit in silence for a long time, looking to Sophie to tell us what to do. She tells Katy it's okay, but her voice is heavy with exhaustion, the weight of yet another betrayal.

So that's why she didn't come back to the room with us on the first night, we say, piecing it together. We didn't realize she had been so drunk.

She wasn't drunk, Sophie says stonily. She's just a bitch.

One or two of us think back to the stories we heard over breakfast the day after that night. The ouzo, the falling over, the sick. But we, as a group, we say nothing.

Caroline and I search the labyrinthine corridors for Molly, to give back her bag and collect the room key. We find her sitting by an emergency exit, her head resting against her knees. She tries to talk to us.

Is Sophie okay? Can I speak to her? Please? I'm sorry, I'm so sorry.

She starts to cry, but we say no and keep our eyes lowered, simply pass over the bag and repeat the agreed-upon line: Stay away from her.

We find the teachers. We explain that Molly needs to be assigned to a new room. Later, we tell Sophie how the teachers went from room to room but none of the girls wanted her. There isn't enough space in here, some said. We don't want her in our room, others said plainly. We wouldn't feel comfortable. The teachers were exasperated. Someone has to take her, they said. They asked the receptionist for another room, but there was nothing available. In the end, she was assigned to a disgruntled pair of first years who regarded her with disdain, as though she was riddled with disease, something they could catch.

We stayed up late that night, trying to make sense of it all. Sophie bought an overseas data package for her phone so she could update her relationship status and unfriend Molly and Leo on Facebook. Her sister phoned, then her mum. We expected her to cry, but there was only a quiet, white-hot fury, shining in her eyes.

What was it? she asked us, her captive audience. Did she have to prove to herself that she could get any guy she wanted? Was it some fucked-up power trip?

We murmured in agreement. It probably was.

She says she was drunk, but so what? She let herself get drunk. She always does – remember my birthday party? Molly chose to put herself in that position. She went to the boys' room. No one made her. No one spiked her drink, did they?

We nod along and squeeze her hand, rub her back.

If she comes near me, Sophie says, I will end her.

We believe her.

The next morning, we eat breakfast on the ship. It isn't as good as breakfast at the hotel in Athens. Fatty bacon and anaemic sausages, cereal like cardboard. We push the food around in puddles of grease, but Sophie fills herself up. She goes back for seconds, eating steadily, ravenously, until her plate is clean. Leo comes down to breakfast late, his hair wet, head hanging like a scolded puppy. He sits on the other side of the room with the boys. We avoid looking in their direction. The ship bobs up and down while we sip our flavourless coffees. We are exhausted, running on nothing but adrenaline and heady anticipation. Through the window, a bright line drawn between sky and sea. We share glances, wondering where Molly is, what will happen when she comes in, where she will sit. What will Sophie do? She would be entitled to tear her limb from limb and stick her head on a stake.

But she doesn't come. We don't see Molly for more than twenty-four hours. We disembark in the midday heat, spend the afternoon walking around Kuşadasi. We buy pashmi-nas and postcards, look at jewellery, ceramics and other trinkets. Sophie doesn't mention her all day, and we don't want to bring her up, so we wait and wonder. We drink cocktails in the tangerine glow of the sun, our group of girls together, turned inward.

Molly appears the next evening. We see her leave the ship, flanked by teachers.

The only people who will still speak to her. And only because they're paid to, Sophie says.

We nod along. Yes, yes, yes.

Maybe she's fucking them as well.

We smirk.

Molly is wearing red shorts and a black T-shirt. She looks like a slut, we say, though the outfits we are wearing are not dissimilar. We pretend she doesn't exist, yet at the same time we are very aware of her presence. It ripples through the group, like a bad smell we are pretending we haven't noticed. We never look directly at her, but we know exactly what she is wearing, how much make-up she has on. When we laugh, we hope she notices what fun we're having. When we whisper, we hope she thinks it's about her. It isn't, but that's not the point.

We climb the steep hill to the old monastery, standing high on the hill of Hora. It is enormous, built like a fortress, the walls over fifteen metres high. Our guide shows us the small opening above the entrance, through which burning oil or lead was poured on unwanted visitors.

They say the screams were terrible, he says. You could see the skin melt from their skulls. It looks like nothing, just a little slit, but it saved the people of Patmos many times.

We move on. We look at paintings of all the miracles performed by St John. Our guide tells us we can visit the very place John had his visions of the final judgement – the cave of revelations.

If you make it there before the sun sets, he jokes. After dark it gets pretty creepy. He gestures back down the long slope, towards the sea, set ablaze by the sinking sun. It looks beautiful; it looks like hell. He keeps talking but we are all looking down at Molly, a shadow, an apparition, slinking back down the path on her own, towards the sea.

That night we dream of fires, of war, of violence and vengeance. The curse of the gods, severed penises, swallowed children, the relentless pull of fate. A fuck worth sacrificing a thousand men; a victory worth a young daughter's life. We wake in our beds, hot, sticky and disoriented. Our eyes adjust to the darkness, and we remember where we are, drifting from one island to the next on an odyssey of our own. The room around us resolves into a simple cabin, each girl in her own bunk, her best friends asleep around her. In the dark, our collective breath is a rhythmic shushing, like the slapping of the sea against the side of the ship, like a mountain breeze whipping through the trees. We rock back and forth, back and forth, buffeted by Poseidon's white-tipped horses, until we fall asleep once more.

The next day Molly tries to give Sophie a note. She corners her in the toilet and says, Please. Please will you just read it. But we crowd her out and tell her no. She's already done enough.

Why doesn't she say it to my face, huh? Sophie says later, when we are back in our room, her eyes hard and wide, her mouth drawn into an angry little pucker.

Sophie has been using her overseas data package to communicate with our friends at home, to make sure that by the time we get back to school absolutely everybody knows what happened. She says she is taking control of the situation. We nod. It is her right.

Apparently now she's saying Leo took advantage of her, she says, rolling her eyes. I mean, please. She wasn't that drunk. She was capable of saying no.

Yeah, we say.

She could have stopped it; she could have said no at any point.

Yeah, we say. Exactly.

It's irrelevant that she thinks she was taken advantage of. It's irrelevant that she was drunk. It doesn't matter who instigated it. *She* went along with it. She needs to shut up and take some responsibility.

Yeah. We can feel a dark, painful aura radiating from Sophie. Yeah, we say. We can't say anything else.

Of course I hate Leo too, she says. But at least he told me the truth.

We nod.

He shouldn't have done it, she says. But I don't know… it's so much worse when a girl does it, isn't it? When a friend betrays you like that, acts like your best friend when they know – she knew – she had betrayed me in the worst way possible. And I mean, you almost expect that kind of thing from guys.

Yeah, we say. We nod. Yeah.

Molly doesn't eat with us for the rest of the trip. We never see her eating, only smoking alone on the deck of the ship, leaning against walls, trailing behind us through the frescoed rooms of the palace at Knossos, or lurking behind a pillar at the Acropolis of Lindos while the rest of us smile for a group photo. There are more countdowns: three, two, one… We smile! We are having so much fun! Her face is as blank as a statue.

We cannot speak to her, of course, but still we are curious, burning to know how it happened, how it really happened. We try to imagine Leo telling her *shh shh*, a sound like the sea, his face a pale moon above hers. We try to imagine her brain shouting *no no no no no no* and her body staying silent. We try to imagine her blurry, slurring ouzo-impaired perspective, her thoughts shunting and flashing, long moments lost to the hazy black hole of alcohol. We try to feel sympathetic, we do. But how hard is it to say no? How hard is it to push back, even through the fog? Had it been us, we would have pushed back, we would not have given in. But it wouldn't have been us. That's the difference between girls like us and girls like her. We never got as drunk as her. We didn't do stupid things like dance in the street or fall over. We didn't have the inclination to stay out late, especially with boys, even ones who were supposed to be our friends. What was she expecting? A sleepover?

And besides, it is so much easier to imagine her smiling coyly at him from across the room, full of intent, brushing up against him at the bar and whispering in his ear. It is easier to imagine her looking up at him through her thick lashes, biting her on her full bottom lip (because her lips are particularly full, aren't they, her eyelashes particularly thick?) and him, rendered helpless by this act, and in the end, under the circumstances, who could blame him?

There was no confrontation, no big showdown like we were expecting, maybe even hoping for. Molly didn't try to speak to Sophie again, and even if she had, we wouldn't have let her. And Sophie, it seemed, truly did have nothing to say to her. It was old news by the time we got back to school. Someone else had done something shocking, something unforgivable, and within a few weeks Sophie was walking around school holding hands with a new boyfriend. Everyone's attention turned to revising for our exams that summer. The trip to Greece became nothing but a washed-up memory.

For a few weeks, we acted as though Molly didn't exist, but slowly we started speaking to her again, when we were in the same classes or drinking at the same pubs. It was as easy as walking through an open door or taking a sip of a drink already in your hand. After a while, it started to feel like maybe what happened wasn't so scandalous. Sophie had moved on, so why shouldn't we? And anyway, at the end of the day, people make mistakes, you know?

But though we wouldn't say it to each other, sometimes, when we are drifting off to sleep at night, when our minds are still and empty, we dream of dark waves lapping against a shore, *shh shh*. A body in the bed next to us, possibilities unspooling like a ribbon of tape from a cassette. In each moment a choice made and a choice taken away. Infinite alternate universes exist briefly before disappearing, crystallizing into hard moments of action, inaction, here, now, something that cannot be dissolved, cannot be wound back, pushing us unstoppably towards an empty beach at night, a bed with sealed exits, a voice in the dark whispering. *Don't say anything, okay? Shh shh shh.*

Chastity

They had been co-workers for about a year before anything happened. Harri joined the company as a waitress but was quickly promoted, first to front-of-house supervisor, then to duty manager. Technically, she outranked Jakob when they were on shift together, but he had been with the company since the start, when there was only one restaurant, and that gave him an unofficial authority. Now there were several restaurants, all across London, and even one in Brighton.

It was Harri's shift that night, a busy Saturday full of rowdy customers, broken glass and endless rounds of 'Happy Birthday'. The team's morale began to wane around midnight, so Harri comped a bottle of tequila and told them to knock themselves out. As she passed a shot to Jakob, he winked at her, and an unexpected shiver shot through the middle of her body. Some people stayed for more drinks after they closed, but before long they began yawning and saying their goodbyes, heading off to catch night buses or meet up with others to continue the night's adventures.

Harri closed the back door behind the last gaggle of wait-
resses and sat down at one of the restaurant tables. She had
two messages, both from Fred.

Hey gorgeous. How's it going? X

Guess you're having a busy one. See you in the morning.
Love you. X

The table was covered with mess: crisp packets, lime
wedges, paper cups filled with cigarette butts. She would
need to wipe down the table again before she took out the
bins and set the alarms. As she rose to fetch a cloth, Harri
heard a tapping sound. It was four in the morning. The
whole front of the restaurant was glass. The bar lights were
on and the street outside was dark – she was lit up like an
exhibit in a museum. Harri froze. There could be anyone
out there at this time of night. She slunk down the side of
the restaurant towards the host station, where the lights
were switched off. There, by the door, a figure. She squinted
and tried to make out their face. All the while the finer
details of the latest rape and murder case marched through
her head. She reminded herself that there was CCTV
throughout the restaurant and a panic alarm by the host
station that could call the police to the restaurant within
minutes, or so they'd been told. Harri stepped out of the
darkness.

It was Jakob, his grinning face pressed up against the
glass. Did I scare you? he said, after she unlocked the
deadbolt.

No.

I missed my bus… Can I wait in here?

Of course.

Jakob opened his mouth to thank her, but something took over. Harri kissed him. He smelled of lime and cold air. Oh, she thought. So this is something I want. After a few seconds, Jakob began to manoeuvre Harri from the restaurant into the kitchen, their lips still pressed together, hands grabbing at each other's clothes.

What are we doing? she said.

There are no cameras back of house, Jakob murmured. Though that didn't exactly answer her question.

Jakob lifted Harri by her waist and put her down on the chrome work surface, shiny and spotless from the post-shift clean. A thought flashed through Harri's head: this is where they prepare food. She felt like a piece of meat in Jakob's practised hands, a free-range chicken whose chest cavity he was staring into, wondering what to stuff it with. She closed her eyes. Jakob nudged his head between her legs. What had she started? She hadn't thought this through. What about Fred? What about Lola, Jakob's girlfriend? Harri pushed Jakob's head out from between her legs and got down onto her knees on the cold tiled floor. She began to unbuckle his belt.

Uh-oh, he said.

She pulled his jeans and boxers down and found, instead of the erect human cock she was expecting, a robot cock, sheathed in chrome, fitted with a tiny padlock and secured around his hips with a chain. Her own distorted face reflected back at her in its shiny surface.

What the fuck?

Jakob bit down on his knuckles and shook his head apologetically. Harri stood up. She felt dizzy. She was cold. Their skin glowed sickly yellow under the strip lights.

What is it?

Well… It's a cock cage.

Can you take it off?

I wish, he said. I don't have the key.

Where's the key?

Lola has it.

Lola? Harri's head was spinning. Is this… Is she worried you're going to cheat or something?

No, no. Nothing like that, Jakob said, pulling up his boxers.

Harri rubbed her forehead.

It's nothing to worry about, Jakob said. It's just a sex thing. You know, she controls how and when I come. Like, power play.

Oh. Harri leaned back against the cold metal surface that still bore the print of her buttocks.

I've upset you.

No. It made me feel bad, that's all.

Jakob pulled her in close and kissed her. I don't want you to feel bad, he said. He slipped his hand between her legs.

Harri thought about resisting – that would be the right thing to do, the responsible thing to do – but she didn't. She let go, and everything else fell away. Harri heard herself asking him to pull her hair. Something had opened up inside her and she was running with it, running, running, through this new, wide-open space and not looking back. She closed her eyes and felt the blood beating around her body, her skin tingling, the physical sensations of being alive.

.   .   .

It was starting to rain. Harri pulled her jacket closed and walked with her head down. Jakob waved to her from a table by the window. They were meeting in a cafe not too far from the restaurant.

Jakob stood up and wiped his hands on his jeans. His hands moved upwards in a strange, flitting motion, as though he was about to hug her but then thought better of it. He clasped them together at his chest. Hi, he said.

Hello.

Coffee?

Yes please. Cappuccino.

I'll be right back.

Harri glanced around. The cafe was empty. The walls were purple, every surface filled with green houseplants. There were a few brightly coloured works of art on display, the kind filled with shapes and squiggles that were supposed to represent something Harri could never see. She took off her jacket and checked her phone. She had to be at work at 3 p.m.

Jakob came back with the coffees. So, he said.

So.

He watched her. Harri met his eyes but had to look away. She felt exposed, like she was being assessed. Her cheeks flushed with colour.

I owe you an apology, Jakob said finally.

Harri added another cube of sugar to her coffee and stirred it, even though it was too sweet already. Jakob waited for her to respond. When she didn't, he continued.

I should explain a few things.

The cafe door opened. They both looked up in alarm, but it was no one they knew. Harri felt like a recalcitrant schoolgirl, waiting to be told off for something she didn't think was her fault.

So firstly, Lola and I have an open relationship. That means we're both allowed to have sex with other people, so –

I know what an open relationship is.

Of course. And, well, as far as I know, your relationship isn't an open one…

No.

So, I'd like to apologize. I shouldn't have… gone through with that, knowing what I know.

Harri pressed her lips together.

I don't want you to feel bad in any way about what happened. I take full responsibility.

Well, how do you feel about it?

The question came out snappier than she'd intended, as though she was telling him off. He smiled, in a slow, infuriating way, as though he enjoyed seeing her like this – nervous, out of her depth. Harri's tummy was flipping over and over, and not, as she had previously thought, because she was scared of being caught.

How do I feel about it? I had fun. But I know it can't happen again.

Harri nodded. She tried to tell herself the heavy feeling in her chest was not disappointment but relief.

.   .   .

Next weekend, Harri and Fred went to a barbecue hosted by one of Fred's friends. The friend had straw-coloured hair and a floppy fringe that made him look like a member of a nineties boy band. He was shorter than Harri, and at least a head shorter than Fred. He wore glasses with round, wooden frames and a small silver hoop in one ear.

Fred, my man!

He reached up to sling his arm around Fred's neck. He didn't acknowledge Harri. Fred looked over the friend's shoulder and gave her a half-hearted smile of apology. She followed them along a thickly carpeted hallway, through a kitchen so white it made her think of the orthodontist's office, and into the garden. It was one of the first sunny days of the year. There was still a chill in the air. Harri wore a blue-and-white patterned dress and a denim jacket. Her legs were speckled with goosebumps.

The girlfriend of one of Fred's other friends came over to say hello. Harri nodded and smiled along, but inside she was smacking herself in the face. The thing she hated most about parties like this was the fact that the conversation never went anywhere but repeated itself, going round and round in a circle like a snake eating its own tail.

By the time Fred found her again, she had been given a Pimm's and lemonade and told at least four people that work was going fine, thank you, then she had listened to each of the four people soliloquize about their own lives for so long – boasting about holidays they'd been on and successes they'd had – that she was amazed they didn't realize how rude they were being. She nodded and smiled and wondered how long they would continue to talk if she didn't say a word.

The host finally introduced himself. Matthias, he said, extending a hand. You must be Harriet, right?

Harri, she said.

Did you ever think about being called Hattie instead?

Did you ever think about being called Matt?

Touché. Matthias smirked at her over his beer. So what is it you do, Harri?

Harri opened her mouth to speak, but Fred jumped in. She's in restaurants, he said. For now.

She hated the way he kept telling people she was 'in restaurants', as though she dealt in them, or had shares in them, as though she wasn't literally there in a real restaurant every single day, counting the grubby notes people paid with, getting down on her knees to wipe up spilled drinks, picking up shards of broken glass with her bare hands.

For now, repeated Matthias. A little something to keep you busy until the wedding, eh? Until you've got your hands full with a crowd of little Freds running around the place?

Matthias chuckled before excusing himself to greet a new arrival. Fred was dragged into another conversation with a friend and his girlfriend. Harri knew she should stay and join in – that was why she was here, wasn't it? – but when she heard 'mortgage rates' and 'our interior design friend', she knew she couldn't bear it.

She walked over to the drinks table and asked for a glass of Sauvignon Blanc, but all they had were natural wines made of grapes she had never heard of. She accepted a glass of the least offensive-looking white wine and walked around the perimeter of the garden, feigning interest in the flower beds.

When they first met, Harri was working as a cocktail waitress. Fred and his friends had come to her nightclub to celebrate. They were boisterous and far too loud. Harri could see the bouncer on his toes, waiting for them to smash something so he could chuck them out, but word had been passed down from management to overlook their antics. Apparently the birthday boy's dad knew someone. Harri had been on her way to their table with a tray full of Jägerbombs when someone walked straight into her. She didn't know if it was one of Fred's group or a total stranger; whoever it was didn't hang around. It felt like she had been hit by a wall – a clean severing of the moment, a flash of light – then she had come round, flat on her back in one of the VIP booths, skirt ridden up, a bag of ice dumped on her head. And beside her, Fred, his eyes soft and unfocused, clasping her hand in his.

Harri often thought of that story as an example of how different Fred was from his friends. How kind, how caring. But at these parties, they were all the same. In the last few years they might have progressed from playing catch with bottles of champagne to discussing their new cars, but it was still showing off, only now with a more adult sheen. At one point, she had been that thing for Fred: his shiny new girlfriend. But since their engagement party, even his most persistent friends had given up trying to persuade her to sleep with them. When she'd first told Fred about their propositions, she'd expected he might get angry, so she gave him a watered-down version of the things they said to her. He just laughed. Even later on, when it got worse, when she told him exactly what they'd said, their beer breath on her cheek in the smoking area while Fred was in the toilet, their hands lingering too long on her thigh at brunch, Fred continued to laugh it off, saying they were chancers but they would never do anything, not with his girl. The possessive made Harri wince. But she didn't say anything. Wasn't she the one hoping he would go out and defend her against his friend's advances?

What are you looking at?

Fred appeared at her shoulder. She was staring into a small, decorative pond, in which it was clear no real wildlife lived.

Hmm?

Lost in a daydream, are you? Fred took her hand. Come on, I want you to meet George's new girlfriend.

In the car on the way home from the party, her insides warmed by those sour glasses of wine, Harri began to feel faint twinges of desire, a string tightening somewhere deep inside her. She looked at Fred, her Fred – his kind eyes, his lightly tanned skin and his easy, affable smile.

She stroked his arm. He looked across the car at her and smiled.

Is somebody a little drunk?

Maybe.

Sometimes she wished he would take advantage of her, or at least pretend to take advantage of her. She wished he would look at her like he was starving, and she was the last plate of food left on the entire planet. When they'd first got together, they had sex all the time. When they were back-packing around South-East Asia, they did little else. They'd make elaborate plans for the day, agree to meet some fellow travellers to see some gorgeous waterfall or visit a temple or a street food market, and at the last minute they would collapse back into bed and spend the day naked, stewing in their own filth, the sun white-hot through the cracks in the blinds. Harri decided that when they got back to their flat, she would go for it, the way she used to back then. She would surprise him by dropping to her knees the minute they got through the door. He would like that. She smiled to herself thinking about it. Then afterwards, maybe he would lift her up in his arms and carry her into the bed-room, throw her down on the bed and give it to her. No, he would go slowly, really slowly. So slowly she couldn't stand it. She'd be moaning and begging him to please fuck her harder, please –

The car stopped and Harri's eyes flew open. The face in her fantasy had changed from Fred to Jakob so quickly she hardly noticed. In the mornings, on her way to work, she had taken to checking Jakob's social media accounts. He didn't have Instagram, only a poorly maintained Facebook page and a Twitter feed mostly filled with retweets. Still, Harri found herself visiting them every day, to see if anything had changed. Whenever there was something, the new knowledge gave her a thrill. Lola was much more active. She didn't use Facebook much, but she at least wrote her own tweets sometimes, and she posted fairly regularly on Instagram. The other night she'd posted a picture of two chicken salads and two glasses of wine with the simple caption: *Dinner*. Harri scoured the picture for details – the nice wine glasses and the trendy earthenware bowl. In the background, a basil plant, a jam jar of pens and a kitchen window that overlooked a normal-looking London street. She wanted to know exactly where they lived. She wanted to know what their kitchen looked like. Then again, maybe the two people having dinner were not Lola and Jakob but Lola and someone else.

Harri and Fred got out of the car and walked into their building. As the lift doors slid shut behind them, Harri imagined taking Fred's hand and putting it between her legs where, maybe, she wasn't wearing any underwear. He would feel how wet she was and look at her with a mixture of surprise and delight. Would they have time to fuck before the doors opened on the fifth floor? She looked at Fred. He was looking at his phone, his brow furrowed. The doors dinged open. Their older neighbour was waiting to get the lift back down.

Good evening, Mrs Brown, said Fred.

Good evening, Freddie, Mrs Brown said.

Harri hated the way Mrs Brown called Fred Freddie, the way she smiled at him, her soggy grey lips spread across the mask of her face. She hated the way he indulged her. It was practically flirting. If Mrs Brown were fifty years younger, she'd have every right to give him hell for it.

Are you okay, baby? Fred said to Harri. You've been quiet ever since we left the party.

I'm fine, Harri said. I've just been thinking.

Yeah?

He put the key in the door. She was trying to decide whether to pounce or whether to wait until they were in bed to start something. But maybe then he'd say he was too tired. Why was she being so indecisive? It shouldn't be this hard, should it? With her boyfriend, the love of her life, her husband-to-be? They weren't even married yet. Maybe she was worried he would reject her. What if she got down on her knees, ready, and he said he didn't feel like it?

Fred opened the door and walked in, dropping his keys into the basket on the little console table in the hallway. He was about to turn into the kitchen when Harri grabbed him, pushed him up against the wall and began kissing him. She pressed her body against his.

Woah, he said. What's brought all this on?

I thought I'd give you a blow job.

What, now?

Yes, now. I'm offering now. Do you want it or not?

Yes, god yes. Of course I do. I was surprised, that's all. I didn't expect this, so you know... Oh!

Fred moaned, a full, deep-throated moan, and Harri felt a shudder ripple through his body. She almost rolled her eyes. Sometimes it felt like he was being a little overdramatic, as though he thought she needed some reassurance that he was enjoying it. She wished he would stop with this performance. Still, she recognized that was a hypocritical thing to think. How many times had she faked an orgasm to get Fred's head out from between her legs when all she wanted to do was sleep? How many times had she groaned, performing pleasure, when she was a little sore and he was hurting her, because she wanted him to hurry up and finish so she could watch another episode of *RuPaul's Drag Race*?

I'm gonna come.

She pulled back.

What are you doing?

You don't want to come now, do you? I thought we could... you know.

Oh, Fred said. I just... I was enjoying it.

You don't want to have sex with me?

What? Oh my god, Harri. I was enjoying the... you know. Is that a crime? That doesn't mean I don't want to have sex with you. In fact, if anything it shows I do want to have sex with you.

Well. Come on then.

Wasn't it possible for them to fuck without bickering? She stalked into the bedroom and started taking off her clothes. Fred began undressing too, in a functional way, as though he was getting ready for bed. He wasn't even

watching her. He wouldn't know if she was doing a strip-
tease for him or licking her own nipples. Fred got into the
bed, under the duvet, and waited for her. For a second, she
thought he was going to pull out his phone from beneath
his pillow, but he was just getting comfortable. Looking at
him there, tucked up in bed like a small boy waiting for his
mama to kiss him goodnight, Harri felt a wave of reluc-
tance surge through her body. She realized the problem was
bigger than this particular occasion. The thought of having
sex with Fred again and again in this bed, forever, with
the lights off, his body moving rhythmically over hers to
the same gently shuddering conclusion, made her feel cold
inside. There had been desire before, hadn't there? They'd
had that spark. There had to be something she could do to
get it back.

Why don't we try something different?

Different how? Fred said, the suspicion palpable in his
voice.

Harri's resolve wavered. I don't know, different like…
Maybe, I don't know. You could spank me.

Spank you?

Yeah. You could slap me a bit with your hand or… your
belt…

My belt? Fred was incredulous. You'd like that?

Yes.

They looked at each other across the room. She, standing by the window, completely naked, lit from behind by
the orangey glow of the street light. Him, sitting up in bed,
looking at her with distrust, as though she had morphed

into a seven-headed demon, or someone entirely different, someone he didn't know at all.

You really want me to hit you?

Not hit me exactly. Just... spank me. You know, it's a thing. People do it.

Not people like us.

Harri hesitated. How did they come to be categorized as people like them? And how had she become a person like that? Was she only included by association with him? What kind of person would she be without him? Just another skint waitress?

Fred sighed. You want me to do it now?

Yeah. If you want to.

He pulled off the duvet and got out of bed. How do you want to do it? he said. Do you want to lie on my lap or something?

No! Harri cringed. Shall we... you know... start, and maybe there will be a good opportunity for it?

Okay, Fred said, and lay back down on the bed.

Harri moved towards him. She thought about getting on top, but she didn't want to have to look into his eyes after that conversation.

Can we...?

Oh, you want to do it doggy style? Fred sounded bored. He entered her quickly, without preamble. There was a sharp stab of pain, and a warm curtain of darkness fell around her. He grabbed her hips and pushed deeper inside her. She closed her eyes.

So... You want me to like, slap you on the thigh?

Yeah.

Fred slapped her gently on the thigh. It didn't hurt at all. It felt like a wet fish.

Could you... A little harder?

He slapped her slightly harder, and it made a satisfying sound, but there wasn't that sting, that sharp thrill of pain she was desperate for. He slowed down.

No, don't stop, Harri said. I want... I want you to fuck me hard and slap me too – as hard as you can. I want to feel it. Don't be afraid.

He thrust harder and made a strangled sound that could have been frustration or excitement.

Yes. Do it again. Harder. Yes!

It wasn't exactly working for her as she had imagined, but she closed her eyes and decided to at least try to make the fantasy work. As soon as she allowed herself to sink into it, the man behind her was no longer Fred but Jakob. She imagined the ropes of muscle in his arms, his shoulders, taut, standing to attention. She imagined his hands on her hips, in her hair, grabbing her around the neck.

Tell me I'm a slut, Harri said, surfacing.

You're a...

Say it.

You're a slut.

Say it louder.

Harri...

Go on. Tell me I'm your dirty little slut.

All right, that's enough. Fred withdrew quickly and sent her toppling over onto the pillows.

What?

What do you mean, what? I should be saying 'what' to you! What the fuck!

Sorry. Harri drew her knees to her chin and wrapped her arms around herself.

She wanted him to tell her that she didn't need to be sorry, that he was sorry and needed some time, but he'd think about it, he'd try again. He'd think about the things she wanted and maybe he'd think about what he wanted too, but no.

I didn't realize this was where we were, Fred said. I can't treat you like that, Harriet. I can't insult you to make sex more interesting for you. I'm sorry. I didn't realize I was so repulsive that you needed something... something like that to get you off.

Oh my god, Harri said, dropping her head to her knees. Her bare skin rippled with goosebumps. Can we please rewind? It was just a... I was just trying something out.

I'm not feeling particularly horny any more.

No, I know, she said. I know. I didn't want to be... I didn't want to make you feel like that. I thought... I dunno. I thought we could spice things up a bit or –

I'm not *spicy* enough for you? Fred said. We're engaged to be married, you know.

Yes, thought Harri. Yes. It wasn't something she would forget.

· · ·

A week later, Harri texted Jakob: *What if I said I wanted to do it again?*

She didn't get a reply for two full days. She didn't want to go into work. What if he was there? What would she say to him? What if he had told other people? She felt as though he had the power to split everything open, like a piece of overripe fruit, and reveal the messy, blackened bits at the centre. She liked feeling whole, complete, unnotice-able. She liked feeling that she looked like everyone else. You wouldn't know she wasn't like every other piece of fruit unless you touched her.

On the second day, Harri was called into the office for a meeting with the area manager, her boss's boss. Harri thought about what she would say. She could flat-out deny anything had ever happened between them, though maybe there was camera footage before they got into the kitchen. Or she could say the message had been intended for some-one else. She could say Jakob had taken advantage of her, that she didn't want to have sex with him then, or any time. She had never been interested in him, but she had felt pressured by him, and so if anyone should be punished, it should be him. They could hardly fire her for sending one message, could they? It wasn't sexual harassment, was it?

Rachel, the area manager, opened the door.

Harri. Do come in.

Rachel was an efficient woman. Even the air around her seemed tightly controlled and packed into discrete blocks. She had long fingernails that were always perfectly manicured and painted in bright colours. Today they were cobalt blue.

Harri sat down on one of two chairs in the cramped office.

Hi.

Listen, Harri, Rachel said. Let me get straight to the point.

Harri inhaled sharply.

You've been working here for... What is it now? Eighteen months?

Harri nodded.

Not long. But in that time we've been consistently impressed by your diligence, your hard work ethic, your reliability and your flexibility. The team loves you, that much is clear. Everything is left spotless and accounted for at the end of your shifts. You've dealt with some pretty big issues on your own, like when we had the flooding last year, that drunk underage customer and the allergy instance. Things many more experienced managers would struggle with.

Rachel raised her eyebrows.

Thank you, said Harri.

Seriously, it's impressive.

Thank you.

Anyway, I wanted to have a little chat with you about where you see your career going. Are you hoping to stay in hospitality? Or are you thinking of going travelling again? Something else altogether? What does the future hold for you? I know this might be a big question to spring on you like this...

Harri nodded. Rachel smiled broadly, and Harri noticed that her bottom teeth were all crooked.

I won't beat about the bush. We've had an opportunity come up. At our new Margate branch. We had a manager lined up to take on that restaurant but, well, for various reasons I won't bore you with, it hasn't worked out. We were thinking of recruiting externally for this role, but then someone mentioned that you might be suitable. We know you're young and fairly new to management, but you've been so responsible and hard-working so far, we thought you might be able to rise to the challenge.

Wow, I... I don't know what to say.

We'd give you plenty of support, of course. There will be an experienced team of duty managers and I myself would visit at least once a week, probably more in the beginning. I know this is a lot to think about – this must feel sudden – but we're working to a tight schedule. The remodel is being finished as we speak, and the big opening is pencilled for two months' time. So we would need to know your answer by next week. I know that's not a lot of time, but please do take all that time to think about it and let us know.

Wow...

Rachel smiled again, crooked teeth and all.

Don't say anything for now, and let's arrange another meeting next week. Let me know if you have any further questions in the meantime. There will of course be a significant pay rise, plus a relocation bonus. I'll send you over an email with the details of the remuneration package so you can have all the information while you think it over.

Harri stepped out of the office. She felt like a baby adult, stupid and indecisive. She wished she was older. She wished she was calm and efficient like Rachel, that she could stop and think about things without everything spinning out of her control. She didn't know what to do. Fred would say no. There was no way he was going to move to Margate. And what? Sell the flat? His parents would kill her. Could she commute? A tiny voice at the back of her mind whispered that she could go to Margate without him. She could start over somewhere new, by herself.

She walked down the street towards Soho Square. The air smelled fresh and clean and damp. The benches were full of office workers on lunch breaks, with burritos and takeaway salads on their laps. The sun was glowing through the clouds in luminous flashes; people laughed. She lit her cigarette and took a long drag. Her phone vibrated. She pulled it out of her pocket.

JAKOB: *I would say tell me when and where.*

They agreed on Friday evening. Lola was out. Harri didn't ask where. Fred was going to one of his mates' birthday drinks in town after work. While she was getting ready, Harri had a glass of wine, which turned into two, then three. She didn't want Fred to find the bottle the next morning and ask why she was drinking wine when she was supposed to be at work, so she took the rest of the bottle with her and threw it into a bin outside the station. Riding the Overground made her feel woozy and slightly sick. Bright sun fractured through the Perspex windows of the train carriage. Chips of light danced across the floor.

Jakob met her outside the station. He was wearing a pair of jeans, a plain grey sweatshirt and trainers. Hi, he said.

Hi.

This was the first time they had seen each other since they'd met in the cafe to talk. Harri thought he had become more attractive since then. She felt her body move towards his involuntarily, as though he was a planet and she was caught in his gravitational pull.

This way, Jakob said, walking ahead of her. She skipped a little to catch him up.

Jakob and Lola's flat was an ex-council flat on the second floor of a block. He tapped a fob to gain entry to the building, then they walked up a set of concrete steps onto an open walkway. Harri found herself inspecting everything – the front door, the doormat, the cleanliness of the floors – to see what new insights could be gleaned into their lives. Jakob showed her through to the living room, while he went into the kitchen to get some drinks. Harri stared at the bookcases, the dining table, the cabinet and the record player that sat opposite the sofa in place of a television. She looked out of the window. Beyond a few treetops, far in the distance, you could see the London skyline. The Shard reaching upwards, the Gherkin beside it, squat and distinctive. She felt very far from home, even though she was on the other side of the same city.

Riesling okay? Jakob placed two glasses of wine on the coffee table and a small painted dish containing some nuts.

Sure.

Harri took the glass of wine but didn't take a sip. She was squinting at the spines of Lola and Jakob's books, wondering what sort of things they read and what this might say about them.

Do you like to read? Jakob said. He swirled the wine in his glass before taking a small sip.

Yeah, she said. I mean, who doesn't like to read?

A lot of people. What do you like to read?

All sorts, she said. She wished he wouldn't ask her questions. Didn't they both know why they were here? Why did there have to be all this preamble, all this conversation?

Tell me, Jakob said, his voice low now and sexy, though they weren't talking about anything sexy at all.

Harri tried to remember the last book she'd read but drew a blank.

Are you all right? asked Jakob.

Yes, why wouldn't I be?

You seem a little tense. I just want to make sure…

Oh my god. You're not pressuring me into anything. I can make my own decisions, you know.

Oh, I know. Jakob moved towards Harri and took hold of her waist. Can I kiss you?

Harri nodded. She thought about how Fred would tell his friends: Harri likes to think she wears the trousers. He would refuse to do what she'd asked, even if it was something like take her home when she was tired and unwell, or stop drinking when he was already too drunk and she knew the night would end with him covered in vomit and her hosing him down in the bath. His friends smirked back. She could see them thinking: Oh, she's one of those girls.

I want you to tie me up.

The words were out of her so quickly she almost wondered if they came from someone else. Both their bodies froze. Harri felt her heart rate ramp up and up until it was less a beating, more a quivering in her chest. She'd once read that the body cannot tell the difference between fear and excitement. The hypothalamus triggers the same physiological reaction in the body, whether presented with something new and thrilling or a threat. *You can choose excitement over fear*, the article insisted. *You can take control.* Harri closed her eyes.

Okay, Jakob murmured.

He led Harri to the bedroom. He removed her clothes slowly until she was down to her underwear, a black lacy set she only wore on special occasions. Harri shivered. Jakob instructed her to lay back on the bed and lift her arms above her head. She complied, watching his face above hers, brow furrowed in concentration as he looped the cord from his dressing gown around the metal bed frame and round and round her wrists several times before tying it tightly back to the frame.

There, Jakob said softly.

Harri tested the knot by bringing her arms forward. It felt pretty tight.

Don't worry. You'd be able to escape if you needed to.

Harri nodded. She didn't trust herself to speak. Jakob stood at the foot of the bed and watched her.

Are you sure you're okay with this?

Harri nodded again. It was her suggestion, wasn't it? She imagined what she looked like from above, a bird's eye view. Semi-naked and bound on Jakob and Lola's monochrome polka-dot sheets. Being this exposed and helpless was equal parts thrilling and terrifying, desire and fear bleeding into each other, becoming indistinguishable. She felt like she could cry, but at the same time she was wet between her legs. Every cell in her body stood to attention, ready and waiting to see what was going to happen next. Fuck me, she whispered. Please, fuck me.

Who was this person, speaking through Harri without her permission? She felt like she was evolving, changing, from the Harri she knew into something – someone – else. Was this good? she wondered. Was this okay? Was that the right thing to say?

Not yet, Jakob murmured. You'll have to wait.

Harri looked down, across the desert of her body, to where he stood at the foot of the bed. His cock was straining against his boxers, no longer locked up. Jakob pulled his T-shirt over his head. He could do anything to her. But wasn't that part of the fun? Wasn't that what made her so excited? He was in control, and she was a pawn in his game.

You can do anything to me, she said. Don't hold back.

What did that mean? Why had she said that? She didn't know, but it seemed Jakob did. Oh, I won't, he said, leaning over, brushing his lips against hers. Don't you worry.

·　　·　　·

The next day, Harri went out for lunch with Fred and his parents. They went to a place in West London, dark green walls, velvet banquettes and crisp white tablecloths. Outside, it was a sunny day, but inside, the low lighting conjured a perpetual evening. During the course of the meal, they discussed the issues the men were having at work. Fred felt he was overdue a promotion – he worked so hard. Fred's dad was having problems with his team. Fred's mother nodded along sympathetically. Harri did the same, smiling and nodding when it felt appropriate. Yes, the wine is delicious. Yes, that fish is exquisite. Yes, Fred truly does deserve more praise. No one asked Harri about how her job was going, and for once she was glad. It was complicated. Was she excited or scared? Both? Neither? There were questions she needed to ask herself, questions about her career, about Fred and about Jakob, but she pushed them aside and allowed herself to wallow, if only for one day, in the memories of the night before. She thought about how, after he had teased her, Jakob had untied her and rolled her body over, taking her firmly in his hands. She remembered how she'd gasped when he was finally inside her, how it felt like she was dunked underwater, into some deep, dark part of herself. The memory of pleasure rippled through her, an aftershock, like a protective wrapping. She felt invincible. Harri marvelled at how she could be simultaneously playing the part of the perfect daughter-in-law and be deep in the memories of another man's body. How ridiculous, she thought. This performance, this theatre. She was both here and not, and no one could tell the difference.

When they finished having sex, Jakob made them toasted cheese sandwiches. They sat on the bed naked and ate them together.

Can I ask you something?

Sure.

If you and Lola are in an open relationship, then why the... you know...

The what?

You know what.

But I want you to say it.

Fine. The... cock belt thing.

Oh, the cock cage?

Harri glared at him. Jakob laughed and kissed her shoulder.

It's something we like. Sometimes I'm submissive, sometimes she's submissive. But when it's my turn to be submissive, I like Lola to deny me. It's hard to explain, but it's phenomenal. It works for us, anyway.

Harri nodded and finished her sandwich. She wondered what it would be like to be the dominant one, the one in control. She didn't think she would like it at all. On the other side of the room, on the top of the chest of drawers, there was a framed photo of Jakob and Lola, arms around each other, laughing. She hadn't noticed they had been watching her this whole time.

In the taxi on the way back to their flat, Fred chatted away. He was going to speak to his boss on Monday and ask – no, demand – the promotion he felt he deserved. Harri looked out of the window at the pale, cloudless sky, the city streets blurring below, and she knew she should tell Fred about her job offer. She should tell him now. She should at least mention it to him. He was her fiancé, for god's sake. They were supposed to talk about things like this. But she didn't. As Fred talked on and on, she felt her mood deflate. What must it be like to feel so sure, so deserving of everything you wanted?

Earlier that week, Harri had gone to visit her mother and sister. Alice still lived at home, or rather at their mother's new home, in the house bought by her new husband, an old Victorian property with large bay windows and a magnolia tree in the front garden, original wooden flooring, and a heavy door with stained glass panels. The day Harri visited, the magnolia had started shedding, its petals thick and brown beneath her feet.

Harri! Alice said when she opened the door. She was still in her school uniform, a rumpled white shirt, her striped tie skew-whiff. I've missed you.

Harri breathed in the familiar sweet scent of her sister, of deodorant and sweat and hairspray. How long had it been?

Her mother was in the kitchen, chopping vegetables for a salad. She had sliced them into thin sticks. Julienne, she said. It's a julienne salad. I thought it would be nice in this lovely weather. Can I get you a drink, Harriet? Some lemonade?

Sure, Harri said, sitting on one of the bar stools around the kitchen island. It felt strange to be here, in this beautiful house, the kind of house she'd dreamed of living in when she was a child.

Her mother passed her a glass of lemonade. Alice rinsed some more vegetables in the sink. The back door was open and Harri could see out into the garden, the table set up on the lawn, spring colours bursting from the borders. Harri had thought about telling her mother or Alice about the job offer, but when they were seated around the garden table, tucking into their salads, it didn't seem like the right time.

Where's John? Harri asked.

Oh, he's at work, said Harri's mother. He always works late. Bless his heart. Always working hard, isn't he, Alice?

Mm-hmm.

And how's Fred?

Harri noticed the way her mother's mind slid so easily from John to Fred.

He's great. I think he's on track for a promotion actually.

Well, that's wonderful. I didn't expect anything less from him, of course. I always knew he'd take care of you. He's a good lad, isn't he? Alice has got a boyfriend now, haven't you, Alice? Did she tell you? I met him the other week. He's a lovely boy.

No, she didn't say.

Alice looked up and pulled a face. I wouldn't call him my boyfriend, not yet.

Well, there's plenty of time for that.

Harri's phone vibrated in her lap. She had a new message from Jakob. She didn't want to know what it said. What would it matter? She remembered the flat she'd lived in as a child with her mother and Alice, the way mould crept up the walls and her mother counted out piles of change on the coffee table to put in the gas meter. The way she and Alice shared a bed with their mother for far too long, using each other's body heat to keep warm. The flat was always spotless, despite the mould, and sometimes they would wake in the night to get a glass of water and find their mother spraying a new home-made concoction onto the mould to try to get it to disappear, for good this time.

She had been kidding herself that she deserved something new, something bigger and better than what she already had. She had been so wrapped up in the excitement of it all that she didn't notice the fear, the very real fear, of everything she stood to lose. She knew then that she wouldn't take the job in Margate. Why would she? She had Fred. They had a future, a real future, with children and houses and holidays and dogs and date nights and everything she could ever dream of. What more could she possibly need?

The car swerved as the driver avoided an oncoming cyclist, who seemed to appear out of nowhere. Fuck, the driver said. Sorry, boss. You okay back there?

No worries, mate, said Fred. We're fine.

Fred looked at Harri across the car, the expanse of leather seats. They were inside a metal skeleton hurtling around a roundabout, joining a dual carriageway and heading home. Harri thought about how they were always just hurtling along in their skeletons, looking for somewhere to go. How stupid it all seemed, all of it.

He reached out his hand. The space between them had never felt bigger, but he crossed it. He stroked her leg in a gesture that felt so familiar, so safe, that it brought her back from wherever she'd been, a place where the world was spinning too fast, like a merry-go-round she couldn't get off.

Are you okay, baby? Fred said. I lost you for a moment there.

Don't worry, Harri said. I'm back.

Margot

Margot and I have been friends since we were eleven, when we wore jumpers two sizes too big and fat little ties which were supposedly cool. We phoned each other most nights. We often ran out of things to say, but it wasn't a problem. We would lie on our separate beds in our separate houses and listen to each other breathing. Friendship meant something different to us then. When I see her now, my insides slide as though I've taken a step and left my body behind. We hug. She smells strange, earthy and sweet at the same time.

You look well, Margot says.

Oh, so do you, I say. It's been so long.

We haven't seen each other in years. I offer her a cigarette, but she's given up. I light up anyway, take a long drag and watch as my smoke drifts across the table towards her, the way her face shifts ever so slightly. We discuss work, the weather, things we've seen on Facebook. That's how I found out about her engagement. I sent her my congratulations and she suggested we catch up. I couldn't say no.

Margot shows me her ring. It is as big and sparkly and green as it was in the pictures. Like my eyes, she says, without a trace of irony.

I wonder if the old Margot is trapped somewhere inside this one. I imagine her head banging against a ribcage, thud, thud, thud.

So beautiful, I say.

Back then, I was the pretty one. But wasn't me who decided. The boys did – those strange creatures with authority on our appearances. They decided who was nerdy or cool, lesbian or fuckable, pretty or ugly. There was no space in between. Our own ideas about ourselves flitted about uselessly but didn't land anywhere; created an uncertainty that left us borderless, undefined. But I had it easier than Margot. I was the pretty one because she wasn't. She was so pale she was practically see-through, the shifting dark mass of her organs almost visible beneath her skin.

We loved playing brides. Funny to think of that now. Sometimes we sneaked into Margot's mother's room to try on her huge, frothy dress when we were home alone. Margot standing in front of the full-length mirror, one nipple poking out of the sweetheart neckline. We used to make collages of our dream weddings. We'd spend hours trawling through magazines and catalogues, our scissors scraping around each chosen image, the remainder collapsing onto the floor. It was such a treat when we got given a new copy of *Brides* or *You and Your Wedding*. One time, Margot's mother gave me a bumper edition of *Elle Wedding* and I thought I would faint with delight. I believed I had it all mapped out. I just had to wait until I was grown up for a man to come along and choose me to be his wife. I couldn't wait to be loved like that.

Margot's voice is soft and even, a line running across a screen. I burn the tip of my tongue on my coffee, press the sore point against the back of my teeth. Everything becomes sharper. I keep nodding, on and on, like a dog stuck on a car dashboard.

You should come and stay with us! Margot says, clasping her hands together. The inflamed skin on her knuckles splits open, red and livid. You'll come for a weekend, won't you?

She looks like a girl again, eyes wide like that. I hesitate for a split second – and I say yes. Of course I do.

Margot becomes more animated, and I feel warm, like I've done a good thing. She chatters on about venues, vows, flowers. She can't wait for me to see the house. It really is beautiful, she says. I feel like all my dreams are coming true.

I don't say *I'm happy for you*. I am curious about her life. I want to meet the man who has chosen her until death do them part. I want to understand how their lives work like that, side by side.

My boyfriend refuses to come with me. I knew he would.

But you hate Margot, he says, lolling on the sofa, watching some mind-numbing reality programme. Girls in bikinis, a sun-spun pool. Sky so blue it's practically neon.

She's my oldest friend, I say.

But you hate her.

I think about saying please, asking again in a cutesy voice, but he'd sulk all weekend and generally be a dick about it.

I do not hate her, I say. He grunts. My body flares momentarily with rage. I squeeze my left hand tightly in my right.

You've outgrown each other, he says from the back of his head. Let it go.

I watch his face side-on in the flickering light and wonder what it must be like to be inside his head. Sometimes I fantasize about scraping his eyes out with a pen.

Go if you want to, he says. But I'm not coming with you.

The night before I'm due to go to Margot's I fall asleep on the sofa with the television on. I dream of one thing, then another, grand cinematic scenes that change abruptly, leaving me reeling. First, I'm sweating, juddering, burningly itchy everywhere. I reach up to scratch my scalp and to my sick horror something comes away, lumps stuck under my fingernails. Something sticky and grey, shining in the moonlight. My stomach slips, swoops. I realize it's my brain, coming out of my skull. Then black. I'm lying down. Maybe I'm in bed. No, not my bed. A bed. Margot, smiling down at me. Long red hair trailing across my chest. There is a blinding light behind her head, so bright it hurts to look at. It darkens her face; I can't make it out properly. But I know it's her. I can tell. I can smell her. I can see her teeth in the blackness, glinting.

It was just a dream, but it's a relief to find my head in one piece. I glance down at my hands; count my fingers to check they are all there. My eyes burn with sleeplessness, and I wish to god I hadn't agreed to this.

I take my boyfriend's car. He'll be comatose all day anyway. Probably won't even notice. I turn up the radio to disguise the strange clunking sounds it makes. I try not to think about how many times I've asked him to get it checked out. Before long, packed motorways give way to winding country lanes. I could be going anywhere. The motion and exhaustion lull me into a state of peacefulness. I put on my sunglasses and imagine I am going on a solo road trip somewhere exciting, off into the sunset, leaving my life behind.

What will Margot and I talk about? I could ask about her parents. I wonder if Margot still sees them. Family has always been an uncomfortable topic for us both. But Margot's mum used to look after me when my own mother couldn't. She never complained. Never said anything about my swollen eyes, my shaky voice. She was always cheerful. Some nights she would wait by the side of my bed until I fell asleep. Sometimes she said it felt like she had two daughters, like Margot and I were sisters. I push it from my mind. That was a long time ago now.

I miss the entrance to Margot's drive the first time. I didn't notice the forest get so dense. Sunlight filters through the leaves and casts everything in a dark, greenish hue, at once calm and inexplicably sad. I smoke before I go in; stare upwards through the branches as though I'll find something in the distant cracks of blue sky.

Margot's voice rings out behind me. You made it!

I did, I say.

There is a pause that feels like a lifetime, and in it I regret being here with every inch of my being.

Come in, Margot says. Let me give you the grand tour.

It turns out that Margot's fiancé can't make it tonight. He's working away, but she hopes he'll be back in the morning. We can take a walk across the cliffs together.

You can see for miles. It's beautiful, she says. All that water.

A memory surges: fifteen-year-old Margot on holiday with her parents in Wales. Grey sky, grey rain, so heavy it hurts. She sits down and screams that she won't go on. We pull our hoods up; wait until she's done. Her face getting redder and redder. Us watching, silent as walls. I ask Margot if she remembers.

Hmm, she says. That was a long time ago.

But you remember?

I suppose I didn't like walks as much back then, she says with a chuckle. I love them now though, don't you? I love being out in nature. Everything smells so fresh. I don't sup-pose you get much of a chance in the city though, do you?

No, I say, and take a sip of wine.

Margot and I didn't fall out often as teenagers. I never liked confrontation. But when others said things about her, I didn't defend her the way I know she would have defended me. I didn't tell her when her period leaked through her knickers and onto her skirt during maths class. I sniggered along with the rest of the class when she stood up to hand in her test. When the boys said she was easy or called her a slag, I didn't outright agree with them, but I did smile along, sometimes share a quick glance with them. It wasn't that I didn't love Margot. I did, desperately, but watching people make fun of her made me feel better about myself. It was one of the only things that did.

Then the boys started saying she let them put their hands down her pants. Margot said it wasn't true, but one time I saw it happening. Margot's face blank, bored even, skirt hitched up around her waist. Whichever boy it was had his brow furrowed, a slip of pink tongue sticking out in concentration. Boys used her to learn the female anatomy before moving onto better things. Whenever anyone spoke to her directly about it, I remained still and silent and looked down at my shiny black school shoes with ribbons instead of laces. I loved those shoes. Afterwards, we acted as though nothing had happened, to the point where now I'm not entirely sure how much of it actually happened or whether I made it up. But I do remember the sour pang in my heart when I realized she was lying to me, as clear and as true as anything.

Margot tops up my glass. I decide to ask about it, super-casual.

She shrugs. I mean, yeah. I hooked up with boys when I was a teenager. We all did.

I wonder who 'all' is. There was only ever me and Margot. The other girls barely spoke to us, but we liked it that way.

We had sleepovers. Just the two of us in the same bed, Margot clinging to me like a limpet. I'd have to peel her warm body off mine so I could get to sleep. We drank undiluted Pimm's together in the park, made our own fun. We dripped it into each other's eyes because we'd heard that would get you drunk quicker. I remember the sharp sting, stumbling, howling with laughter, clutching onto each other, a life raft in the spinning world. Flashes of those days come back to me. Pissing in the subway late at night when we thought no one was looking. Smoking weed behind the library with boys from another school. The taste of fire clung to my throat, made me nauseous. Walking home in the dark, Margot crept along the pavements, hiding behind cars, insisting someone was watching us, as they always were.

I ask Margot over dinner. The memories are filling me now. I blurt them out, one after another. I want to remember them, relive them. She looks down at her steak and cuts a precise slice, perfectly pink inside.

I don't remember it like that, she says. Perhaps it was the vodka in my eyes.

Pimm's, I think but don't say. It was Pimm's.

So how long have you been with your boyfriend now? She looks at me across the table, and I feel the years we've spent apart stretching between us like a black hole.

More. Getting caught showing each other our privates in the toilet at school. She must remember Mr Muhammad's face. She must. His glasses steaming up, the way he turned pink, stuttering. We were put into isolation for two whole weeks and when our parents asked why he simply said, 'inappropriate behaviour' and coughed into his handkerchief, refusing to elaborate. Flashing our tits to a stranger to earn ten quid for vodka lemonades at the rugby club. I felt so dirty afterwards I couldn't sleep. I let Margot hold on to me all night. Stealing mascara and nail varnish from Boots. Almost getting caught but outrunning the security guard, our hands clasped tight the whole way.

You don't remember any of it?

I don't remember it like that, no, she says, shoving her steak in her mouth hurriedly as though it's about to get up and walk off.

All of a sudden, I want my boyfriend, more than I have in months. I want to be cuddled like a baby. I want to be tucked in bed, to sleep with the light on. I want to be far away from here. I take a long sip of my wine. Edges soften. I feel myself getting drunk. I think I should go, I say.

Margot looks at me. No! she says. No, don't go. Oh god. I've upset you, haven't I? I'm sorry. I didn't mean to.

No, it's nothing to do with you, I say. I just don't feel well. I've got this headache.

You're lying! she says, dropping her cutlery onto her plate with a clang.

I'm not, Margot, I just –

Oh come on, she says. I know it's been a few years, but bloody hell. I still know you.

My heart starts to clang in my chest like an alarm bell. My breath skips, stutters. No, really, I say. I don't feel well.

Don't go, she says, grabbing hold of my wrist. Please. I don't want to be alone.

Instinctively I snatch my arm back and she collapses onto the floorboards with a thump. She starts to wail, and something cracks inside me.

Too much. There's a reason I forgot those years. Each memory folded, unfolded, smoothed out in a different light. Margot's breath hot in my ear: I wish you were dead. Margot screaming in some unspecified place, different places. Blame, blame. Rain-soaked hair, dark smudges under her eyes. Margot jumping out in front of my car when I was on my way to a different friend's house. Her face shivering white in my headlights. Don't do this to me, she says. I need you. I don't want to unlock the door, but I do, of course I do. I'm so young, seventeen, eighteen. I don't know what's happening. There's blood all over her arm and it's so red and she's telling me she wishes I was dead. And then, and then. She's holding me, telling me she'll be okay, and she forgives me this time. Threat hanging in the air like smoke, choking me. When I look in the morning there are bruises up and down my arms, bluish-grey, lilac, mauve, the ghosts of Margot's fingers. You're making this all about you, she says, but I'm the one who needs help. Margot's mum, eyes red, passes me a cup of tea. She doesn't mean it, she says. She loves you.

I wish love was different. Imagine another life. Imagine a dress. Every night I pray she'll get better, that she'll forgive me. Every morning I pray I haven't done something wrong. I think it is my fault. I think it is normal. I think this is just what it's like. Slammed doors, hospital wards. Constantly told: she loves you so much, no need to make a fuss. Tears, tears, tears.

Please stop, I say. You're hurting me, Margot.

You're hurting me more, she says, eyes full of anger, hate even.

There's a reason I forgot so much.

·   ·   ·

When I wake, it is still dark. I am in Margot's bed, but we are not touching. I watch her as she breathes beside me. She looks almost peaceful. In, out, in, out. I think: she is just a person, just one person.

I wonder what her fiancé will make of all this, then I get it. Slowly at first, then all at once. This house is beautiful but bare. There are no photographs, no pictures of any kind, very few personal effects. Margot is as much a guest in this house as I am. I walk barefoot across the polished floors, softly softly, onto the main landing. There are so many closed doors. I don't know which one to choose. I leave them all and take the stairs. I float out of the front door and leave it open. Why not? I take a deep breath of cold air. I am surprised to find there is no voice in my head telling me that it's all my fault. I stare up at the fuzz of stars beyond the treetops, the clear sky above.

One more. Summer. I'm standing at the edge of the jetty, looking at the rush of green water beneath my feet. All the other children are splashing and laughing, but I'm afraid. What if I sink and drown? What if I get eaten? What if there's seaweed? I take a step back.

There's nothing to be afraid of, a voice says behind me.

I turn around and there she is, long red hair dripping down her back, her breasts barely two puckers on the flat board of her chest. She takes my hand and smiles.

You just close your eyes and jump. One, two, three.

Road Trip

I have been waiting almost an hour when my mum's car pulls up outside the station. Her white Prius stands out among the black cabs, a swan in a huddle of ducklings. I see her through the car window, pale hands on the wheel, brow furrowed as she scours the concourse, wondering why I am not waiting in the agreed-upon location. My phone starts to vibrate in my hand as I reach the car. I open the passenger door.

Hi, I say.

Where have you been? she says, barely glancing at me, her mouth drawn in a knot.

I came down from the platform when I saw you arrive.

My seat belt clicks closed. The car smells of clean leather and my mum's heavy, citrusy perfume. My stomach lurches.

You said you would be waiting here.

Yeah, well... you said you'd be here an hour ago.

She checks the rear-view mirror. You're starting already, are you?

Starting what?

This… This thing. She takes her hands off the wheel to wave them about. This bad attitude, the sulking, whatever you want to call it. You know what? Just don't today, okay? Just don't.

I say nothing. Ordinarily I would say something. I would raise my voice against hers until we were both shouting. Me, about how she came to be an hour late and didn't manage to send a message or make a call – doesn't she know how it feels to be abandoned like that with no answers, waiting and waiting? And she would tell me to get a grip, Allie, just get a grip, making me feel small and wild and uncontainable. The whole cycle runs through my head, a familiar routine of shouting, words flying back and forth like tennis balls, but I'm too tired to start it off. I sink back into my seat and look out of the window as we circle back past the station and the people I've been standing with for the last almost-hour: the homeless couple with their dog and a coffee cup of change on the ground in front of them; the cheery guy who tries to tempt every passer-by into taking a free session at the gym.

I take my phone out of my pocket and plug it into the car's charging point.

Oh no you don't, she says. I need that.

But you're not using it right now.

But I will need it – look, I'm only on thirty-six per cent.

I'm on one per cent! I say, waving my phone at her.

It's my car! she says. You can't charge your phone.

Fuck you, I say in my head, but not out loud. I take back my phone and fold my arms. I look out of the window at my ghostly reflection racing along the wall opposite, through the trees, faster and faster as we take the road that leads out of the city.

She doesn't ask about what I did last night. I knew she wouldn't, but still I hoped she might. I would have got a thrill from saying 'not much' and letting her dig for information, eking it out as slowly and as irritatingly as possible. When I left yesterday evening, I told her I'd probably be back that same night. Some small part of me thought she might have worried when she woke up and I still wasn't home.

My phone flashes with an incoming call: Mattie. My heart keeps time with her name. Mattie. Mattie. Mattie.

Mum glances over. Your phone's ringing.

I can see that.

Her eyes widen. Here we go.

What is your problem? Mum snaps. I came all the way out here to pick you up and now I'm asking myself why. Why did I do you a favour? Why did I bother driving out here on a Saturday morning to pick up such an ungrateful girl who thinks the whole world revolves around her? I've got news for you, Allie. It doesn't. Next time you can walk all the way home, or get the bus, or hitchhike for all I care. Are you listening to me?

Yes, I say. I'm listening.

She could talk about my flaws for hours. I'm too much of a dreamer. I am completely devoid of empathy. I'm ungrateful. I'm dirty. I'm always late. I am a bad daughter, a bad friend. I wind people up on purpose. I'm impolite. I don't use my cutlery properly. I say certain words in a stupid way. You would think after hearing it so often there would be no impact.

Mum drives too fast, swinging around roundabouts and barely slowing at junctions. Even when we are in slow-moving traffic, she jiggles her leg up and down and pulls off with a jerk every time the car in front of her moves more than a centimetre. Sometimes she gets like this, anxious and wound up, full of energy like a bomb that's about to go off. I don't think it's me this morning, though I didn't do anything to improve her mood. It's probably her boyfriend, Mike. Last time they had an argument, she threw a drink at him and he said he would never come back. Somehow it became my fault. If only I wasn't so difficult. If I could just answer her questions with full sentences. The following afternoon, when he showed up on the doorstep, she was all smiles, like nothing had happened. I watch her face, the clenched jaw, the frequent flaring of her nostrils.

What? She turns to look at me, her eyes hard stones.

Nothing, I say, looking away.

Then stop staring at me.

She turns the radio on, loud. I look down at my feet in my scuffed Converse trainers. Once they were white, but now they are a dull, dirty grey. I am trying not to think about last night. What will I tell Mattie? I should be drafting an apology or an explanation, but I can't push the images of Reena and Max out of my mind. They were still asleep when I left, semi-clothed and peaceful on the sofa, the cold early morning light pooling on their skin. I think about the curve of Reena's neck, her mussed hair, Max's pale chest and soft hands. My face is too hot. My heart is a fist thumping thumping thumping against my chest. The motion of the car makes my brain swill around in my head, smack against my skull.

Can you pull over? I shout, over the music.

Are you kidding me?

She looks over and sees my face: grey-green, studded with sweat. I try to hold it in, take deep breaths and focus away from the nausea and think about something, anything else, but my body takes over and starts convulsing on its own. I clamp my hands over my mouth.

Don't you dare! Mum shrieks, as though she can control my bodily functions by shouting.

The car swerves onto a grassy verge just in time. I open the door and bile rushes out of my body. I tremble and blink back tears. Mum is still yelling at me. Everything is shimmering slightly, in an underwater way. I struggle to make out what she's saying. She's repeating my name: Allie. Allie. Allie. I try to turn around in my seat and look at her, but everything hurts. I can't. The ground swims in front of me, patchy brown grass, in and out of focus. I cry harder, snorting and sniffing, nose streaming like a hysterical child, but then Mum is shaking my shoulder, pushing me out of the car.

It all happens so fast. My knees make contact with the dry ground. The sun bursts out from behind a cloud. Mum's face in shadow, hard and twisted. She shouts words I don't hear, lost to the roar of passing vehicles. The door slams.

She's gone. At least I have my phone, I tell myself. I press its buttons, willing it to light up, but it is dead, a useless weight in my hand.

At first, I just lie there. The ground spins, and waves of nausea crash over me. I think about what would happen if I died here. Would Mum feel bad? She would, I know. The guilt would eat her alive. Not because she would miss me or anything, but because then she would have to live the rest of her life knowing she was a bad mum, that she had failed, that there was no chance of absolution. What about Reena and Max? They don't deserve to feel guilty. Last night was my fault. I'm always taking things too far.

The sky is wrapped in thick, unmoving cloud. Cars speed past as though nothing has happened. Lives continue. I imagine a child in the back seat, gazing out of the window.

Mummy, why is there a girl lying on the ground by the road?

Don't be silly, darling.

I close my eyes, and we're at my grandparents' house. Thick, brown carpet. Yellow-and-brown patterned wallpaper. A wall-mounted electric heater. A taxidermy ferret, baring its teeth at me from the display cabinet. I am six years old. My grandma makes me spaghetti bolognese and lets me watch VHS tapes while the grown-ups talk about grown-up stuff. I'm watching *The Raggy Dolls*, the same three episodes I always watch. My grandfather slams his mug down on the table. Tea splatters the carpet.

I said no, Catherine.

Please, Dad. You might not want to leave, but she has a life of her own to live, outside these four walls –

Stop this, please, my grandma says, her voice wavering, her eyes pink and watery.

You don't have to stay here, my mum says. You can come with us.

She's not going anywhere!

I let out a panicked sob, a dart through the air. Everyone looks at me as though they have no idea who I am.

My grandfather throws his hands into the air to dismiss us all. Grandma flinches. He puts on his thick glasses and picks up a book from his reading table.

Mum, my mum says, a note of desperation in her voice. Mum, please.

Just go, Grandma hisses. Please, go. You've done enough. Her cheeks are flushed red, her breath shaky. She leaves and doesn't look back. She leaves without saying goodbye to me, something she has never done before.

Dad, Mum says.

You heard your mother, my grandfather says, not lifting his eyes from his book. It's time for you both to leave.

When we get into the car, I am still crying. It is dark outside, my mum's face illuminated in the soft blue light of the dashboard.

What happened? I say after a while.

My mum doesn't say anything. She doesn't even look at me. Her eyes remain straight ahead, watching the road, as though she hasn't heard me speak.

Is Grandfather a bad person? I whisper.

She laughs. We're all bad people, Allie, she says.

I absorb this information. Everyone?

Yep.

Even me?

Oh yes, she says, turning to look at me for the first time since getting into the car. You're a bad person too. I've seen it sometimes, behind your eyes.

Both my grandparents are more or less gone now. Grandfather died of liver cancer when I was eleven. Grandma lives in a care home. When Mum and I visit, she mumbles nonsense, made-up words, sometimes smiling, sometimes shouting, sometimes crying. We know it's time to leave when she starts telling us about the bad man, saying he's waiting in her room or hiding out in the garden. Mum rolls her eyes. The carers laugh. Don't be silly, darling, they say. There's no bad man.

A few months ago, I asked Mum if she remembered saying that to me. She laughed as if I had told a hilarious joke and said, Well, you were probably being bad. I said I didn't think I was. She said I was probably remembering it wrong.

.   .   .

I don't know where I am exactly. At least a twenty-minute drive from home – but how long will that take me to walk? If I leave the main road, I might find a village, a small cluster of houses, maybe a shop. But what if there's nothing but yawning emptiness? Country lanes leading to more country lanes. I wish I'd paid more attention to the road signs.

Something Green, Little Something, Something Heath. I sit up. Pain flashes through my head like a gunshot. My throat is dry and sour. I know there's a petrol station along this road somewhere, I've seen it from the car. After a few minutes, the trees that line the road flatten into fields. Then, just before the roundabout, a Texaco garage pops up, a brief splash of red. There might be a payphone or a phone charger I could use. What else can I do?

Last night. I didn't mean to stay out. I promised myself I wouldn't. But after spending a couple of hours in that same pub everyone in our year goes to, the only place that accepts our fake IDs, I couldn't bear the thought of going home. I hadn't had any fun yet.

Do you wanna get out of here? I said to Mattie. We could go somewhere else?

I don't think so, she said.

But I'm bored.

I stirred the remains of my extremely overpriced Archers and lemonade and knocked it back. I didn't even feel slightly drunk.

Mattie, baby? I stroked her arm through the soft material of her cardigan.

She didn't look at me.

Don't make me go without you.

I'm not making you do anything.

I squeezed her hand under the table. I know you want to come with me. I know you do.

I don't. I'm having a nice time here.

But what if you could have a nicer time?

She shook her head and turned away from me to carry on talking to Aimee and Karim about their philosophy teacher.

I just love everything about him, Aimee was saying. Even the weird shoes he wears. They make me think of elves –

Ohhh, you like that? said Karim. You're into some weird shit!

What? No, I'm not into elves! I'm just into... him.

And the cardigans, Mattie chipped in. On anyone else it would be a weird old man vibe, but on him it's like, hello sexy librarian.

Aimee and Karim murmured in agreement.

But the question is, said Karim, is he into men or women? Who among us mere mortals stands a chance with the devastatingly gorgeous Mr Taylor?

Definitely women!

Both?

Nah, let me tell you, he's one hundred per cent gay. It's that hair...

I watched Mattie, the way she fiddled with her necklace when she was listening and clamped her hand over her mouth when she laughed. She'd changed a lot since she first moved here two years ago. Back then she was a mess, always saying and doing the wrong thing, but I liked her anyway. Now she looked more or less like everybody else.

I texted Max: *You out tonight?*

He replied within a few minutes: *Yeah. Come to the Ship. Reena's here.*

I looked around the table. People were smiling and laughing. Someone was asking if anyone wanted to split another rum and Coke. Two girls were taking selfies. Someone was reading out a Twitter thread and asking someone else *Can you believe it?* I watched them all, my friends, with reverent sadness, as though I was leaving and never coming back.

Mattie looked up as I rose from the table. Oh, are you going?

You sure you don't wanna come? I looked at her, my gaze hard, as though I could burrow my way inside her head. *Don't make me beg.* She shook her head. Why wouldn't she come with me? I felt a sizzle of anger in my belly, but I pushed it down. I didn't own her. She could make her own choices.

Where are you going, Allie? asked Aimee.

Just to meet some other mates for a bit.

Ooh, she has other mates! said Karim.

I'll see you guys on Monday, yeah?

Mattie wasn't looking at me.

I bent down to give her a kiss on the cheek. I'll call you tomorrow.

Yep, speak to you then.

A chorus of 'byes' followed me out the door. I didn't need to look to know Mattie wouldn't be one of them. I stepped out into the cool night air. I imagined what it would be like if she ran out now and joined me: her cheeks rosy, hair messy and all over her face. The way she always looked slightly sweaty but in a good way, as though she had recently finished dancing or having sex. She was always warm; she was her own source of heat. I felt a sudden wave of sadness that she wouldn't come with me, that we wouldn't have fun together. I shook myself out of it. You'll see her tomorrow, I told myself.

There was a security guard on the door at the Ship, but he let me inside with barely a second glance. It was suspiciously easy. I had been psyching myself up beforehand, so the sudden release nearly made me laugh out loud.

Max kept bringing me foaming columns of beer, even though I told him more than once that I didn't like it much. You'll take what you're given, child! he said loudly.

Everyone at the table erupted into giggles and shushed him. The sheltering of an underage drinker was a game, a secret mission. I was less than a year younger than some of them, but there was a hard line between seventeen and eighteen. They were all on one side, and I was on the other.

As well as the beers, we had a few shots, and Reena gave me lines of coke off the back of her iPhone in a toilet cubicle. I didn't know her particularly well – both Reena and Max had been a couple of years above me at school, but now they were both on a gap year: she was interning at a magazine; he was working in the kitchen at Nando's, supposedly saving up to go travelling – but the three of us had started to gravitate towards each other at parties, the way people who take drugs tend to, united by the fact that our other friends raised their eyebrows at us and got frustrated by how long we spent in the toilets. We pooled money and contacts, shared a rolled-up note or a cut-off straw. The fact the three of us were together meant the night was always going to end a certain way. The bell rang for last orders, and when everyone else disappeared into cabs and onto last buses, Max picked up a couple of grams of mandy.

We decided to go back to Reena's. Max insisted. He said Reena's house was so big that even though her parents were home, they wouldn't be able to hear us. Reena rolled her eyes but didn't contradict him. We went downstairs to the basement, the room Reena called the 'snug'. The word 'snug' is so casual and intimate, I was expecting some sort of cosy den filled with books and games, a couple of armchairs squashed together. I was not prepared for the spacious room with its high ceiling, velvet sofas, deep brown parquet flooring, expensive-looking rugs, artwork displayed on the walls in tasteful, asymmetrical arrangements. At one end of the room were French windows that led onto a small, stone courtyard; at the other was floor-to-ceiling walnut panelling. Reena pushed one and it popped open to reveal a counter full of bottles of spirits, and underneath, a number of temperature-controlled wine fridges. I tried to take it in my stride, but the secret door was too much.

Holy shit, I said.

What? said Max with a smirk. You didn't know Reena was rich?

Reena blushed, a mixture of pride and embarrassment creeping over her face. I'm not rich...

Max was rummaging in the bar. Yeah, I mean, how many of these do you have at home, Allie? He pulled out three enormous bottles of champagne.

What the fuck are those?

Oh, Reena said. They've been in there for ages. We can drink them if you want.

Max pulled out a small baggie filled with powder. A magnum of champagne and some mandy, he said. Now that's what I call a party.

You're not putting all of that in, are you? Reena said.

Abso-fucking-lutely, Max said, winking at me. You're gonna be hammered by the time we've finished this.

After that, the night breaks down into fragments, images, words. The pop of a cork. The three of us dancing breathlessly to music videos, Reena and me draping ourselves over Max like the women on the screen. The sour chemical tang of the warm MDMA-infused champagne hitting the back of my throat. I can't remember what order things happened in. But it was probably me who took my clothes off first. I'm always the one who escalates things.

.   .   .

Cars roar past, whipping up great gusts that judder through my body and make my teeth chatter. I imagine the people inside looking out and I wonder what they think about me. Occasionally a car slows as the occupant tries to get a closer look – a flash of fear – but I tell myself no one will harm me here. It's the middle of the day. There are too many witnesses. I'm on display, something interesting for drivers and passengers to look at, something to break up the monotonous landscape: trees, fields, repeat. I could be seconds away from a car losing control, skidding and flattening me, but still, the fear of being kidnapped, raped or murdered is more acute. It fills me with a humming dread. I think of Mum, at home now, perhaps with Mike. Is she thinking of me? I should be angry with her, and I am, but more than that I am tired. My anger rages in the same detached way as my fear. I stand outside of it, watching it, aware of it, but not feeling it.

I have no idea what time it is. What difference would it make anyway? It's not late enough that I'm worried about not making it to the Texaco before dark. No one is expecting me anywhere. No one is expecting anything from me. I'm adrift in time, or non-time, like a stick floating down a stream. I walk past one of those emergency SOS phones on the roadside. I've never seen one up close, but good to know, I suppose, that if I was in danger there would be some way for me to contact people who could help. I imagine racing down the road, someone behind me, snatching up the handset and screaming: *Help!*

How could she leave me on the side of the road? It's a hollow thought. She told me I was pathetic once, her eyes filled with a hate that crushed my insides like a Coke can, made it difficult to breathe. What had I done? Something she didn't like, ignored her messages or the persistent phone calls that never seemed to stop, said something stupid or embarrassed her by showing up at the office, where she sits straight and stoic, unsmiling, dressed in her cold-coloured suits – metallic grey, pale morning blue – face hard and impenetrable.

One time I went into the big office in the city when I knew she was there for a meeting, to ask her for money. She had already told me no at home. I'd spent quite a bit that week. I thought I'd confront her and make it impossible for her to say no. She wouldn't want to look like a cheapskate in front of her colleagues, would she? She gave me fifty quid in cash, and a long, hard smile. When I returned home the next evening, I opened the door to the porch as usual, but the inner door was bolted shut. My key slid into the lock, but it stuck there. It wouldn't turn. Through the frosted glass window, I could make out a hazy glow of light in the living room and the flicker of the television screen. If I strained, I could hear voices, a dramatic swell of music. She was watching a film. I jiggled the key and I called to her. She didn't move. At first, I thought she couldn't hear me. I called a little louder, banged my fist against the door and rattled the handle.

Mum! Mum, it's me!

I tried her phone. No answer. I tried the back gate: locked. After a few minutes of banging and shouting, of wondering, was she on the phone? Was someone else in there with her? Had she somehow gone deaf during the day? I realized. I went cold, like someone had tipped an ice bucket into my chest cavity. After about fifteen minutes I saw her blurry shape go into the kitchen to get another bottle of wine. I sent her texts: *PLEASE let me in. I'm SO sorry. I will NEVER pull a stunt like that again. I LOVE you. PLEASE PLEASE DON'T DO THIS.*

After two hours, she started turning off the lights downstairs. I called to her again.

Mum, please let me in! I'm sorry.

I thought she would open the door once she had finished her film. I thought she wouldn't be able to sleep knowing I was out there in the dark. But it wasn't until the dull, grey light of morning, when the birds had begun their incessant song, that she finally opened the door. Get inside, she said to the crumpled heap of daughter on the tiled floor, in among the shoes and umbrellas.

I shuffled inside, grateful for the warmth. Perhaps I should have kept banging and shouting, louder and louder, until a neighbour or a passer-by noticed. But even then, what could they have done? Called the police? Broken down the door? But it ran deeper than that. On one level, I didn't think anyone would help me. Why would they? And on another, I didn't want to draw attention to myself, I didn't want anyone else to see how little my own mother cared about me, because what does that say about what kind of person I am? How bad do you have to be to be rejected by the person whose body was your first home?

The patchy roadside of dust and wispy grass gives way to lush, verdant green. Trees reach up from the earth for about fifteen minutes – barely ten seconds in the car – then, as quickly as they arrived, they disappear. The roadside becomes gravel; small, chalky white rocks underfoot. There are fields again, a distant horse or two. They seem far away. A metal barrier appears; I must be getting close to the garage. Vehicles slow, brake lights flashing like angry eyes. And there it is. A red T looming, shimmering, a mirage on the horizon. I don't run towards it. I don't even pick up speed. I continue at the same slow pace, wondering what I will do, what I will say. How should I respond when I am asked where I am going, why I am out here on foot and why I need a phone charger? The thought of saying words, forming sentences, feels like an impossible task.

There is a cafe beside the petrol station that sells coffee, burgers, breakfasts, that sort of thing. I check the menu in the window. A laminated piece of A4 paper, Comic Sans font. I don't have enough money for anything. I sit on the kerb outside. My feet hurt. My head is swimming. Now the rhythm and aim of walking is gone, the pain is back. Options weigh heavy in my skull, but I can't formulate them into decisions and actions. I drop my head to my knees and close my eyes, take small, shallow breaths. *Do not vomit. Do not vomit.*

Are you all right down there?

I don't know how long I've been hunched over. A man stands before me: tall, slightly stooped. He is wearing thick-rimmed glasses, full head of brown hair like a brush.

I'm fine, I say. Thanks.

You don't look fine.

I squint back up at him. He is smiling at me knowingly. What does he know about me?

What do you want me to say? I ask.

He looks thoughtful, turning over what I've said as though I have made a fascinating philosophical point. I almost expect him to stroke his chin.

Would you like to join me for a burger? On me, of course.
You can choose whatever you like.

My stomach grumbles a response, but he can't hear it
above the traffic. Horns beep in the distance. I desperately
want some food. I want to eat. I want to sit down for a
while and think. But I also know I shouldn't accept gifts
from strangers.

No, I'm okay, thanks.

Come, he says, not missing a beat. I'm not going to
kidnap you. I just want to see you fed.

He laughs, as though kidnap were a hearty joke, and
as he laughs I see the dark cavern of his mouth, raw meat
red. I consider accepting his offer, then I see him see me
thinking about it and hate myself for being so weak, so
transparent.

Come, he says again, decisively. What would you like?

He tells me his name is Damien and he is the father of
two young boys, three and five. He tells me this quickly, in
order to show off his credentials, I suppose; to reassure me
that he won't hurt me. But I already know there are many
kinds of parent. I order a double cheeseburger with fries and
a black coffee. Damien goes for pancakes with bacon and a
cup of tea. He dithers over whether or not to order a vanilla
milkshake, before deciding it would be too sweet with the
pancakes as well. I stare at him. He's sweet enough already,
he tells me with a wink.

Damien eats slowly. He cuts his food into small, precise shapes before placing them into his mouth. He tells
me about his job as a history teacher at a local sixth form

college. He talks a lot. I relax. He watches me over the rim of his glasses. There's a strange expression on his face, as though he can see right through me, to the veins and the bones and the muscles beneath my skin. I wait for him to mention his children again, or his wife, but he doesn't.

Do you have a boyfriend, Allie? he asks softly, out of nowhere.

I start. I don't remember telling him my name, but I must have. I tell him that no I don't, and it feels like a betrayal even though it's true. Mattie. I close my eyes and try to conjure her face, but I can't. She has become distant. Even Reena and Max feel faraway, like people I will never see again. I think of them waking up together in Reena's snug, embarrassed, regretful. But they are friends, they love each other. They will talk about it and laugh and become comfortable around each other again. Last night will become a fond, if slightly awkward memory. Life will go on and I will be outside it, looking in.

Damien gets the milkshake in the end. We have been sitting together for nearly two hours. He brings me back a Coke.

I thought you could use the energy, he says, smiling.

When the light starts to fade, he offers me a lift home. I haven't told him where I live yet. I accept, a sense of dread and inevitability unfurling in my brain like a fog. It was always going to end like this. As we walk towards his inconspicuous silver people carrier, I feel my body become stiff, as though my soul has left and is hanging around somewhere above me.

Once both doors are shut, he puts his hand on mine. I look down at his hand, thick with hair. Mine, beneath it, looks small and unsubstantial, like a doll's hand. Except a doll wouldn't bite their nails. A doll's nails would be perfect. Mine are red raw and dirty. I pretend the hand I am looking at belongs to someone else. It is easier than I thought, stepping out of myself, abandoning this physical body. I watch him rub the hand gently. Maybe this won't be so bad. Maybe I'll simply disappear.

Here you go, he says.

I blink. In his other hand, he is holding my phone, fully charged. The word WELCOME appears on the screen slowly, as though it is floating to the surface of a murky pond.

Try not to lose it, he says, winking again in that awkward way of his. Text someone and let them know you're in the car with me, yeah?

He starts the car. I come back into myself with a dizzying snap. The radio comes on, some old song, and Damien starts to hum along. I thought… what had I thought? I switch my phone back on, and the notifications pile up. Facebook, Instagram, WhatsApp. Nothing from Mum, nothing from Mattie. I pretend to type out a message, as if someone cared where I was.

You take care of yourself now, Allie, Damien says as he drops me off at the end of my road. It was lovely to meet you, but in the nicest way possible, I hope I don't meet you again. He chuckles, his eyes serious over the top of his glasses.

Thank you, I think. Thank you, thank you, thank you.

The front door is open. My mum and Mike are sitting on the sofa, a bottle of gin on the coffee table, a couple of wedges of lime and tiny, empty cans of tonic water.

Oh, there you are, Mum says. I was wondering when you'd get home.

She is looking at me and waiting for something. My body rushes with adrenaline, the ghost of anger. I wonder if I will cry, but I don't. I think about telling her the truth, then I think about telling her I was forced to have sex with an old man in exchange for a lift home. But I know she wouldn't care. She would laugh and say *Wow, is there anything you won't do to avoid walking home?*

I was about to go and look for you, she says, turning back to face the television. Wasn't I, Mike?

Mike looks at me, but I don't meet his eyes.

I go upstairs and lay flat on my bed. It felt like I was never going to get home, but now I'm here, I realize I was always going to make it back safe. Mum knew it, so why didn't I? I made it back, I tell myself, as though it is something to be proud of. I made it. I want to call Mattie and tell her everything. I want to tell her about Damien, what I thought was going to happen. I want to tell her about Max's hand on the small of my back last night in the pub as he told me to drink up. The way later on he and Reena merged into one body in the dark. I want to tell her about how I imagined Damien was going to grab me across the car and that I wouldn't have been disgusted or even surprised, but willing. He had been so nice. *You won't believe what happened to me…* I would say, as though I am a passive observer of my own life, as though I didn't make the choices that led me here. I remember the glance Reena and Max shared with each other last night, just before. That glance caught and scraped inside me, like a stone lodged in my throat. I stare at the plastic glow-in-the-dark stars stuck to the ceiling. Only a few remain now, scattered fragments of light. Will Mattie be angry with me? Will she even care? Perhaps she won't be surprised. Maybe she didn't come with me last night because she knew exactly where I'd end up. Everyone always seems to be a few steps ahead of me.

My phone lights up with a new message from Reena: *Hey mate, how you feeling? You coming out tonight?*

I probably shouldn't. I close my eyes and feel the bed spin out beneath me, remnants of the night before clinging to my blood. I should get some sleep. Tomorrow is Sunday. I will have to speak to Mattie at some point, and I need to figure out what I'm going to say. I will go with Mum to the care home, I always do. I think of the clinical smell, the whole place dreary, sucked of colour and energy, a waiting room for death.

On the way, we will sit in the car, and we won't speak. I will watch the world outside blurring through the passenger side window. Mum will keep her eyes on the road, focused. This is a kind of limbo too.

Look, Mum will say. Do you remember when we went to Edinburgh together? Do you remember the castle?'

Grandma will laugh. Is that you? she'll say, looking at the photo and back up at Mum in disbelief. Oh right.

Yes, Mum. And that's you.

Grandma will turn to look at me. I don't know what she's talking about, do you? she'll say. I just got here, so I didn't know something was happening and now…

Mum and I will hold our breath. It will go one way or the other. Good or bad. Happy or sad.

I haven't seen you before in my life, Grandma will say, laughing. But you can tell me the story if you think she'll like it.

Mum will take a deep breath and tell Grandma a story about herself.

The Mirror Test

The glass in front of us shimmers with our own reflections. Saturday shoppers scurry past. A busker, packing up his saxophone. An older Christian woman pushing flyers into hands, insisting that it's not too late, it's never too late, Jesus will always be open to you. I shift in my seat and look down at my legs in their thin black tights. If I arch my feet, my thighs appear small and slender, the fatty parts pulled under, concealed by gravity. When I let my feet drop, they spill over the seat like goop.

Someone is watching me. I turn to see a family hovering behind us. Four of them: a toddler on a hip, another clinging to his mum's trouser leg, an older child holding a wobbling tray packed with Happy Meals and cardboard cups of milkshake. The mum gives me a tight smile. I respond with what I hope is an apologetic smile. Sorry, I want to say. I wish I could but... The woman doesn't move. I break eye contact and swivel my chair back towards the window, away from their expectant faces. The table in front of us is strewn with the remnants of our own (Happy) meal: stray fries, half-empty pots of sauce, toys still sealed in their plastic packaging. I pick up my drink and slurp the watery dregs through a straw. We are still consuming. We have a right to be here. When we chose these seats, we knew they were coveted. The three comfiest chairs – one green, one red, one blue – right in the window, perfect for watching, or being watched. We knew we would have to defend them.

Niamh is painting Skye's nails violet with the new polish she swiped from Superdrug. I've seen how she does it – slips small tubes and jars up her sleeve and secures the cuff with a hair tie. One time, the alarm went off. Beepbeepbeepbeepbeepbeepbeep. I wanted to run, heart splintering in my chest, palms slick. I looked across at Niamh. She was smiling at me, the security staff, the sales assistants, as she proffered her bag. She cooperated. In the end, her bag wasn't checked at all. The gesture was enough to reassure them of her innocence. Everyone dispersed as quickly as they had arrived, full of smiles. Later, she shook out her sleeve, spoils tumbling like coins. We all got a new eyeliner.

Skye yawns and examines Niamh's handiwork. Rihanna's 'We Found Love' is playing over the speakers. Niamh is humming along, over the sounds of children screaming, crying, parents raising their voices, McDonald's employees shouting order numbers. A group of boys a few years younger than us huddle around a screen, watching something and laughing.

Skye scowls and picks up her phone carefully with the freshly painted hand. She begins to scroll.

Brandon's going to be there tonight, she says.

I watch the upward curve of her lips, the barely percep-
tible smirk. The black speckles on her upper eyelid where
she didn't wait long enough for her mascara to dry. Niamh
looks up.

Are you still into him, Melissa?

I shrug. Yes. Maybe. I don't know. No.

I won't tell him, you know, says Skye.

She would.

I know, I say. It's just… it's complicated.

Skye opens her mouth as though she might like to say
something else, but then her eyes drift towards Niamh's and
her mouth closes. She turns back to her phone and resumes
scrolling.

Suit yourself.

· · ·

I am looking at myself, always looking, in whatever surface is available to me. A phone screen, a mirror, a train
window, the slick surface of a passing vehicle. What is it
I see? Another person, a glimmering double, living her life
in cold, shiny surfaces. Detached from a body, a mind, she
is only an image. Long hair, full lips, thick lashes, clear
skin. She smirks at me. She is confident, bold. I imagine
heads turning in her direction, boys burning with desire.
They square up to each other. They're going to fight it out,
they're going to hurt each other, and it's all because of her.
She is cruel and detached; she watches without feeling.
It is true people hate her – that's the price she pays – but

their envy, a weight, also lights her up. It makes people look. Even when the mirror shows me someone else, someone messy and imperfect, with blackheads sprinkled on her nose, a sore spot forming just below the corner of her mouth, burst and scabbed, chin too square, arms too hairy, even when I know I'll never be beautiful enough, when the fundamental structure of my face seems incompatible with any kind of beauty, when I feel unlucky to be born in this body, this thing I can tweak but never change, not completely, even then I want people to look at me. I want to be seen.

Melissa?

Skye and Niamh are both looking at me, giggling.

Huh?

We lost you there, Niamh says.

You were away with the fairies.

In the mirror, my cheeks glow like embers. I looked too much; I got caught.

We are at Skye's house, getting ready for the party. Niamh pours vodka from a small glass bottle into our plastic cups of squash. She stows the bottle carefully in her bag. Skye sits cross-legged on the carpet, staring straight at herself in the full-length mirror, tilting her head this way and that. She widens her eyes. She pouts. She is completely oblivious to – or uninterested in – me, watching. In the background of the frame, I catch sight of myself staring. I turn away and look at my own face in a smaller mirror. I review the parts of my face indifferently, as though they belong to someone else, or no one at all. A project, something to work on. Generic features on a diagram. I apply mascara carefully, making sure I don't poke myself in the eye with the brush. I have sensitive eyes, and I will cry and ruin everything, and then I'll have to start again. I apply concealer and watch my imperfections disappear. I apply lip gloss. When I am done, I smile at myself in the mirror: mouth wide and wet and shiny, eyes looking back at me, lashes long and pretty. I wonder, briefly, how much my friends and I differ on the inside, the parts of us we can't see. Which of us has the smoothest femur, or the reddest heart? We know nothing about these parts, sealed up in the liquid darkness of our bodies.

I'm in the mood to get completely trashed, Skye announces. I'm just in that mood.

Don't worry, says Niamh. We'll look after you.

Don't you want to get trashed with me? I want to jump around and sing at the top of my voice and kiss a stranger. I can't do that by myself.

Melissa will get trashed with you, won't you Melissa?

I smile. I laugh. I don't know.

Niamh and Skye's eyes meet across the room, drawn to each other like magnets, and they burst out laughing. I feel cold, cold, cold, like my insides have been flushed with ice water. I smile. I laugh.

Skye's wardrobe is covered with images: magazine cut-outs of fashion models and pop stars Blu-Tacked alongside postcards, Polaroids and strips from photo booths. The largest image is of the three of us. It sits inside a flimsy frame that reads SADIE'S SWEET SIXTEENTH! along the bottom in a curly font. Behind us, a bunch of pastel-coloured balloons; gold chain curtains shimmering. None of us look at the camera. Skye is on the left, in a silky black dress. She's laughing at something. Her hair is set in perfect golden waves. She looks across the shot, at me on the right, or maybe at Niamh in the middle. Niamh's hair is smooth-straight and falls over her face like a curtain of dark water. She wears a maroon crop top and a matching tight skirt, an intricate web of gold chains across her neck. Her eyes are half-closed. She faces Skye and laughs at the joke, whatever it is, her arm around Skye, pulling her closer. I am on the right, also grinning. I try to read my own expression, but I can't. I hardly remember being there, as though the whole night happened to someone else, someone who operated my body, as though I left it on autopilot. We are bathed in the glow of the flash, light reflecting from collarbones, cheekbones, foreheads, shiny, shiny hair. Snap!

I think about the morning after Sadie's sixteenth and how Niamh texted the group chat asking:

Was I okay last night??

And how we responded within minutes, telling her she was brilliant, she was fantastic, she was fun, she was cute, and she had nothing to worry about.

I hope we play spin the bottle tonight, says Skye, looking at her face with her phone camera. She smiles at herself and takes a photo. Niamh rolls her eyes.

What?

You're such a slut.

I am not! says Skye in mock outrage. Okay, maybe a little bit. But in a good way. Sometimes it's fun to let go, you know? Anyway, I'm not a *real* slut. Not like Charlie Morris.

Oh no, definitely not like Charlie Morris.

I laugh. We laugh together. Niamh barks like a dog. *Woof woof woof!*

Charlie Morris. I keep smiling and try not to think too much about what happened to her, or what might have happened to her, anyway. She crawls into my mind sometimes when I read news stories about women who accuse famous men of rape – like that teenager and the footballer in the hotel room, and how they got all her previous sexual partners to testify that she liked it rough, even though I thought they weren't supposed to do that any more – and I wonder. Charlie Morris was drunk, they nearly always are, and it's so stupid because everyone knows you have to get drunk enough to be fun and funny, but not drunk enough to make a mistake or have a mistake made on you. Which is basically the same thing, isn't it?

Before we leave for the party, we look at ourselves in the mirror, our three faces squashed in beside each other. We are all smoothed out and refined: bad parts erased, good parts coloured in and accentuated. Skye takes out her phone. Flash! I am slightly drunk, pleasantly drunk but not too drunk. Our faces smear into one, and I feel quiet inside.

·   ·   ·

Skye's dad drives us to the party. In the car, my phone flashes with a call from Tomas. I let it ring out.

ANSWER THE PHONE NOW.

The girls are singing along to the radio and taking it in turns to sip 'squash' from a bottle. Skye dabs gloss onto her lips in the front seat. We briefly catch each other's eye in the mirror before she looks away. Niamh's eyes are closed as she sings along to Beyoncé and tries to reach the high notes. Everybody is laughing. Everybody is having fun. I ball my hands into fists and belt out the lyrics to 'Halo'.

On the seat beside me, Niamh sways from side to side, hands in the air. In the front, Skye takes out her phone to film us. We wrap our arms around each other and croon.

Tomas didn't want to break up, then I didn't want to break up, but in the end, we both agreed. Whenever we talk about it now, I cry, which he assumes means I want to get back together. But I don't know how to explain the tangle of love and sadness, the desire to be together forever and also to never see him again.

I try not to, but slip into thinking about how Tomas had sex with another girl and I stayed with him anyway. I guess I wanted to win. I wanted to prove I was better than this other girl, the one who slept with my boyfriend as if it was no big deal, as if I was no big deal. I wanted to prove I was it: I was the one. When I told Niamh, she rolled her eyes and told me I was being dramatic. I wait and wait for it to feel less of a big deal, but I still feel dramatic about it. I try not to think of it at all, but I can't stop. I think about it all the time. I imagine Tomas: he picks up this cute girl and pushes himself inside her over and over and over and I try to stop this playing in my head but I can't I can't I can't.

She goes to our college, and even though we don't have the same classes or the same friends, sometimes I catch a glimpse of her moving down a corridor or purchasing a Diet Coke from the cafe and I think about all the ways I could hurt her. I could spill a hot tea on her from behind. I could say it was a mistake, but she would know. She might be burned for life – a scar from me, forever. Or maybe I could corner her in the toilets. I could grab her by the hair and flush her face. I could spread rumours about her on social media, in real life. What else could I do? I could do anything at all. I stare at her as she walks past every day. I will her to look up and see how happy I am, how carefree, but she never does. I look so often that I memorize the sharpness of her collarbone, her delicate nose and her dark eyebrows. Her hair is so straight and shiny I can practically see myself reflected back in it. Sometimes, on particularly slow afternoons, I look down at my notebook and see I have sketched her face in blue biro. Her body, too. Her breasts, her waist. I imagine her naked body all the time.

When I told her Tomas and I had split up, for good this time, my mum asked me if she was sure there wasn't anything I could do to fix it. She asked me again and again. Had I thought about making him a card? Had I asked for a chance to explain? She said it was a shame. She sighed. I could tell I'd let her down.

Skye's dad pulls over in front of Lizzie's house. It's quiet. An orange, liquid light spills out from behind the curtains. He tells us he will be back to collect us before twelve.

Just like three Cinderellas, he says. You shall go to the ball! But if you miss the stroke of midnight, you shall turn into pumpkins!

Dad.

Skye opens the car door, and we follow suit.

Wait, says Skye's dad, leaning over the passenger seat towards where we are all standing together in the road. Come here. Skye. Look, all joking aside, don't leave this house, okay? There's been some stuff in the news... Some unsavoury types, you know...

Dad, for god's sake!

Skye moves to shut the door.

Skye Louise Underwood, don't you shut that door!

Niamh and I turn away tactfully and listen to the hissing sounds of Skye and her dad exchanging words in the front of the car. A compromise is reached. Skye's dad waves at us out of the car window before driving away, his smile tight.

What was that about?

It was nothing. You know dads. Always worrying about nothing. Skye rakes through her curls with one hand. Shall we?

There are a few people sat around in the living room. Ellen is on the sofa with her boyfriend, and there's a group of boys we know drinking beer and talking to Lizzie's brother enthusiastically about what games he has on his games console.

You're not playing video games at a party, Lizzie says.

I know. You've told us already.

As Lizzie turns to show us where to hang our coats, one of the boys says something and the rest of them snigger, even Lizzie's brother. Lizzie doesn't say anything. She doesn't flinch or give any indication she heard them at all. In the kitchen, there are two different types of beer and a few alcopops. There isn't much.

My brother isn't eighteen yet, Lizzie explains. And this is all my parents would buy me.

Do they know you're having a party? Niamh says.

Well... It's not a party. It's more like a gathering.

Who else is coming? asks Skye.

I look at the photos and notes stuck to the fridge. A photo of Lizzie and her brother in school uniform. Lizzie must be six or seven, her front teeth missing, her plaits messy and her fringe stuck to her forehead. She has the biggest grin on her face.

God, Lizzie says. Please don't look at that.

A takeaway menu from the local Chinese restaurant, with three dishes circled: chicken chow mein, egg fried rice and prawn toast. An expensive-looking wedding invitation, on heavy white card with gold detailing, inviting the family to witness the marriage of John and Susanna. A couple of fridge magnets from holiday destinations – Disneyland Paris, Sydney and Mallorca – and a photo fridge magnet of Lizzie, her mum and her brother on a log flume ride at a theme park. Lizzie's brother sits at the back with his arms stretched wide and a contented grin on his face. Lizzie's mum in the middle, wearing a navy raincoat and looking terrified. At the front, Lizzie is bent so far forward, it isn't possible to see her expression, just a blonde ponytail attached to a navy raincoat that matches her mother's, and her arms holding on tight, bracing herself for what is to come. Niamh nudges me with her hip.

Did you hear that?

What?

Tomas is coming.

So?

So? So... nothing. I was just letting you know.

That's all over now. It's not a big deal.

Okay. Do you want some wine?

I didn't know they had wine.

They do. We walked past her parents' wine rack on the way in. Didn't you see it under the stairs?

I accept the wine. My phone vibrates in the pocket of my jeans. Tomas calling again. My heart, my brain, a static fuzz. What is he doing? Is he drunk, is he high, is he angry? I wonder if Tomas thinks I've had sex with someone else. That's what he thought last time he got like this. Endless phone calls, mysterious texts. He'd heard something from someone and he wanted to know, he just wanted to know. He felt he had the right to know.

Niamh and I return to the living room. Nobody asks where the wine has come from. Skye is talking to Lizzie's brother. He has a girlfriend, but we don't know her. Skye arches her back, her breasts extended towards him like an offering. She is laughing more than usual, her face softer in the dim light. He looks at her chest while she speaks. She looks at him looking at her chest. She doesn't seem to mind. Someone has put on music. Drums, guitar. It's loud enough to drown things out.

Do you wanna go outside? says Niamh.

I shrug. Okay.

We go out through the back door and onto a patio. There are white plastic chairs by the door, but Niamh sits on a low brick wall that separates the patio from a long section of grass that stretches way off into the darkness, further than I can see. The air is clear and sharp. We can see the stars, those impossibly tiny pinpricks of light. Niamh offers me her cigarette packet.

What was Skye's dad on about?

What?

When Skye's dad was leaving and he was talking to her about, you know, unsavoury types or whatever. What was that?

I take a cigarette and roll it back and forth between my fingers. Niamh lights her own cigarette and motions for me to lift mine so she can light it for me.

Oh, I say. Well, there's been some stuff in the local news. You know, someone got raped in Palmer Park a few weeks ago.

But we're miles from Palmer Park.

I take a drag of my cigarette. I don't want to state the obvious, that rapists aren't animals who lurk in the bushes all day. They're people who go home, live lives, move on, attack again elsewhere. Lightning never strikes twice and all that. But it's easier to imagine that Palmer Park itself is unsafe, because then the danger is pinned down, easy to avoid. I remember, as I always do when I think about that assault, how it feels to walk down that dark road by my house, beside the train tracks. The small stretch the street lamps don't cover, the nearest houses still a few metres away, just beyond shouting distance.

There was a flasher outside the girls' school too, I say.

A flasher?

Yeah.

Like someone who flashes their penis at you?

Yeah, I guess so.

That doesn't sound like a big deal, Niamh says.

I shrug and laugh, a tinkling sound, coins dropping into a glass bottle.

If it happened to me, I'd probably just laugh, she says. Or else I'd be like, put your prick away mate.

Yeah. I take a sip of my wine, take a drag of my cigarette. I make the right sounds, laugh a bit more.

The article about the flasher was in the local newspaper. Children walking to school were forced to look at this random man's genitals. I imagine him opening a long, dark coat and shouting *Surprise!* I imagine him turning away and unzipping his jeans, as though he was going for a wee in the bushes that line the path, before turning and shouting *Surprise!* I imagine the penis, flopping, dangling, swinging from side to side from its dark nest of hair. Though it probably wasn't soft, was it? I imagine it rising up, transforming, like some terrible monster. One article said he masturbated in front of one of the victims, a twelve-year-old girl on her way home from school after a late detention, a girl the same age as Niamh's little sister. One parent was quoted: *Very hard to explain to my child why this happened to her, and*

I hope no one else has to explain to theirs. I wonder what
I would do if it was me, if I was alone and a man appeared
in front of me like that. I see him smiling, leering, his eyes
sparkling with a challenge, a threat: *What are you going to
do?* Would I freeze, like a small animal caught in a bright
light? Would I run? Would I find it funny; would I laugh?
Would I tell all my friends about my interaction with this
weirdo? Or would I keep it to myself, worried I'd be the
wrong one in their eyes, that it would be my fault, just
for looking?

TOMAS: *Are you at Lizzie's?*

There's no 'x' at the end of the message, which shouldn't
mean anything, but it does.

ME: *Yes, I heard you were coming* ☺ *See you soon.* X

Tomas is typing…

And then he's not.

I pass Lizzie on my way to the bathroom.

Are you all right, love? You don't look too good.

Yeah. I just need a wee.

I edge past her and push into the downstairs toilet, a
bright white room filled with harsh light. The bulb above
my head hums. There are no windows. I lock the door, pull
down my underwear and sit on the toilet. I listen to the soft
hushing sound as my pee hits the bowl. I wipe and stand to
wash my hands. I look at my face in the mirror and it's like
there's no one in there at all. I had forgotten I was attached
to a body, a face. The face does not belong to me. The
teeth that are ghostly white, the faded lips, a hint of purple

wine stain. I splash my face with cold water and open my bag, take out all the items that will help me become more myself. I scrub my lips with a wad of balled-up tissue paper until they are raw and swollen, scar-pink, and I start again from scratch.

. . .

Something has happened between Lizzie and Skye. Niamh and I hear shouting from upstairs, followed by someone sobbing. Ellen's boyfriend comes out to tell us our friend is upset.

I just thought you should know... he says.

Neither of us moves. He goes back inside, shaking his head. We look at each other. We both know Skye is our responsibility, but we don't want to get in there and medi-ate the situation, whatever it is, unfolding between her and Lizzie, the host of the party, the person whose house we are in. The crying quietens a little and we both shrug at each other as if to say: She'll probably be all right.

Niamh's lips are black now from the wine, a similar colour to her hair. It looks so soft I want to touch it. Her skin glows pale and blotchy. I lean towards her. She looks unwell. I hope she's feeling all right. I think this, but I don't say it. I'm laughing at something she's said.

Okay, so tell me, Niamh says, grabbing hold of my arm and whispering loudly in my ear. How old were you when you... you know?

We both cackle, but I don't know why it's funny.

Fifteen. I've only done it with Tomas.

Bullshit! Niamh says, a little too loudly. A knot of people standing by the kitchen door look over at us. I was twelve, she adds in a whisper.

It's not bullshit! You can ask Tomas!

I'm not going to ask him that.

Well, you can. It's true.

Whatever! Niamh's eyes slide in her face. Don't you want to know who my first was?

Niamh never wants to talk about the people she's slept with, so we never ask. Presented with the possibility of this knowledge, I shrink away. Both her hands grip my forearm. I try to shake her off gently, but her grip tightens, as though she's worried I'm going to get up and run away.

Okay... Who?

Oh, it was no one important. Someone on holiday, I think. Hey, Liss... Do you think people think I'm a slut?

Of course not! I say. Why would anyone think that?

But I know people do. No one has ever said it to me personally, but I've overheard them. The boys, they've said horrible things, and the girls... they say much worse.

Maybe... Maybe I am?

Niamh is making a strange grunting sound, somewhere between laughing and crying, and I look around, wondering if there's anyone who can help me with her. We haven't been out here long – we've drunk more or less the same amount of alcohol. How did she get this drunk?

Niamh, I say. You're not... You're not a slut, okay? Let's get you some water.

But I had *sex* when I was *twelve!*

Niamh, shh, I say, pulling her towards me. It's not a big deal.

Why? Why should I shush? Are you embarrassed of me? Are you embarrassed to be friends with such a slut?

I imagine everyone at the party is looking out at the two girls in the garden, clutching on to each other by the arms as though they're holding each other back. One of them is shouting the word 'slut'. The one who isn't shouting looks towards the house – the gauzy curtains in front of the French windows, the silver blinds in the kitchen, even the closed drapes upstairs – but no one looks out.

Hey, come here. Come here.

I wrap my arms tight around her. At first she struggles, but then she gives in and collapses on my shoulder.

Melissa, Niamh sobs. Melissa.

It's okay, I say. It's okay.

Her body is unfamiliar against mine. She's too long, too full of sharp corners. We shift uncomfortably. Niamh was the last one of us who needed a night light at sleepovers. She never wanted to watch any scary movies, not even the ones we were allowed to watch. But now she'll watch anything. The ghost movies, the monsters, the slashers. Sometimes, when I'm hiding beneath a blanket, I peek out and look at Niamh's face, stony and expressionless, the action sparkling on the surface of her eyes.

The back door opens, and people spill out into the garden. Skye is among them, her eyes dry now, her arm looped in Lizzie's. Tomas is there too, hanging back with his friends. And Brandon. My stomach flips. Neither of them looks at me.

Oh my god, says Skye, dropping Lizzie's arm and rushing to Niamh's side. What happened? Is she okay?

She's fine.

She doesn't look fine, someone says.

She is.

I'm fine, Niamh mumbles into my chest.

Do you think I should call my dad? Skye asks over the top of Niamh's head, her eyes round and glassy.

I shake my head, but before I can say anything, Niamh stands up, almost knocking me off the wall.

We don't need your fucking dad, all right?

Woah, hey... Brandon steps forward. Niamh, hi. How are you?

I'm fine. I'm fine. How many times do I have to tell you all? I'm absolutely fine!

Okay, okay. That's great. Look, shall we get you some water? Brandon tries to put his arm around Niamh's shoulder and lead her towards the kitchen, but she pushes him off.

I don't want water. I told you, I'm fine.

You don't seem fine, calls Matt, one of Tomas's friends.

Hey, can somebody stop her from shouting like that? Lizzie's brother says, poking his head out of the kitchen door.

Who's 'her'? Who are you talking about? Niamh asks. Are you talking about me? I'm here, you idiot. Why don't you ask me yourself?

Lizzie steps in front of her. All right. Listen to me. That's enough now.

Don't, I say. Lizzie, just leave it.

This is my house! I'm not going to have her screaming like this in the garden. What the fuck happened to her?

Well, fuck you and your precious house. It's a stupid house anyway.

Niamh starts laughing.

I wouldn't want to live in this stupid house... I'd rather live on the... on the street!

Hey, hey, Niamh. Come on. That's not nice.

Brandon is still trying to play the peacekeeper, his arm hovering above Niamh's shoulders in case he has to grab her. Me, I'm holding her hand, trailing behind. There are too many people talking now, people talking about Niamh, people talking to Niamh. Other people talking about other things, I guess.

I don't care, Niamh says. I truly don't care any more.

Well, get out then. No one wants you here, anyway, says Lizzie.

Lizzie! says Brandon. Come on –

What? She's ruining my party! Niamh can start shouting like that about how I have a horrible house and... somehow... it's all my fault? I'm just trying to make sure everyone has a nice night.

I didn't say that.

Lizzie's brother reappears. Hey... Hey, buddy. How about you don't upset my sister at her own party?

Brandon holds his hands up. Just trying to help... Forget I said anything.

The garden has filled with people, everybody is looking

at Lizzie now, the mascara-flecked tears slipping down her cheeks. People gather round, ask her if she's okay. I watch them all milling about, checking in on each other in the aftermath of the drama. After a while, I realize I can't see Niamh anywhere. She let go of my hand. I didn't even notice.

Niamh? Niamh!

Where did she go?

I turn to look for Skye. She's there in the hallway, with Brandon. His arm around her. Their heads bent close together. He reaches out to touch her cheek and she smiles. I freeze. It dawns on me slowly, like peeling back the wrapping on a present I already know I don't want.

Oh shit, Skye says. Melissa…

I turn back towards the kitchen. I can't. I can't deal with this now. I call Niamh's name over and over again, even though it's obvious by now that she's not here. She's not in the house. She's gone.

Skye is standing by the front door when I walk through it. Brandon is in the corner, looking at his feet. Skye says my name. I don't look. I don't want to see her sorry, sodden face. I don't want any of this. Skye, Brandon, this party, this body, any of it. I just want to find Niamh.

Melissa, please, Skye says. We should call my dad, we really should.

I laugh. Excuse me, I say, as I push past her. Did she believe her dad would be able to save us, every single time?

Niamh. Outside, the sky is black but filled with endless specks of light. It's cold. My breath blooms white in front of me. I shiver. I left my jacket inside. Never mind. I take out my phone to call Niamh, and when I look down at the screen the letters shift and slide across the screen. Maybe I am more drunk than I thought. Niamh. Behind me, I hear someone open the front door. Without turning around or thinking about what I'm doing, I start to run.

What do I look like, running like this? Down the road, across the playing fields. I can't hear anyone following me but still I run, I move, the air so cold, so painful in my lungs that it gives way to a sharp, pointed kind of pleasure. I think of Niamh, what she told me. I remember her, twelve years old, the same age as her sister, Eimear, the same age as the victim of the flasher (the paedophile, the sex offender, the pervert), the same age I was when my periods started, the smudge of thick brown in my underwear. I knew it was coming, I wanted it to come. I wanted it so much, but if I'd known, truly known, what it was like, I would have waited forever. All the things we don't talk about creep out of the woodwork of my mind, all the things we keep secret. I think about how I want to touch myself – no, how I *do* touch myself – when I think about Tomas fucking someone else. It turns me on even though I hate her. And then I hate myself even more, filling up with sadness and shame when I come, sheets twisted in my fingers. I think about how our history teacher adding Skye on Facebook and calling her Little Bunny isn't the joke we all make it out to be. I think about the marks on Niamh's arms, the ones she says are caused by her cat scratching, scrabbling out of her grasp. Light pink, red, scabbed over, blood. Stop.

Niamh! I yell. I'm down by the river now. Niamh, please! My voice disappears into infinity overhead. House lights blink on the other side of the water, shiver in its black surface. I don't stop.

Tomas called me a slut once, a good little slut, and it felt like a compliment. I stretched out, still and naked, on his bed, waited while he viewed me through his screen, moved the parts of my body to get the best shot. My head buzzed with static, white noise, car alarms. When he was done, I sat up and pulled the sheets over my chest. I watched him survey each photo. My body spread, posed. His face quiet, inscrutable. You need to show me you love me, he said. I said I did, I did, I do, still do. He found new ways for me to show it. (Knees aching, caked in mud, jaw aching, dirty slut.) I stared at myself in the mirror and tried to find the bold girl glimmering there, in the mirror's shine, the one I thought I was, but I couldn't see anything at all. My face so still and silent, my reflection disappeared. A wisp, a breath. But the noise in my head was so loud. Tomas's friends called me insatiable and said he was a lucky boy. I thought that was something to be proud of. I wanted to be wanted. I wanted to be someone's prized possession, a precious object. I wanted that flickering, quivering power. I grasped at it again and again, and still it slipped through my fingers. I trailed behind like a ghost, on the outside of the joke. It was all good humour; they meant no harm. I didn't let on that I felt any pain. He loves me. He loved me. He would do anything for me, anything to keep me for himself. I must feel so special. Don't I? Don't I?

Melissa!

There she is: Niamh. Standing further up the path like an apparition. I rush towards her. I need to tell her. I need to tell her everything. Does she not know? (Did I not know?) Or do we know but never say? Do we think it's kinder (better, nicer, easier?) not to say anything at all? I sprint. I think I'll catch her. I think I'll tell her, right now. I'll tell her everything. She catches me in her open arms, holds me tight.

Don't, she says. Don't say anything.

In the morning, we will wake up and feel that crushing sense of dread for what we were about to do or say, or what we did do and say, and we will wish we could take it back. We will look in the mirror and wonder how others saw us: screaming, crying, composed, beautiful, ugly, whore, nothing at all. But no matter. We will let each other forget. We'll clean up together. I'll message Niamh and ask if I was okay. And I know, within minutes, she will tell me I was fine, I am fine, everything is completely fine.

Niamh takes my face in her hands.

You're a mess, Liss. You've got mascara all over your face.

Yeah, well.

At least you're not a slut.

Oh, stop it. You're not a slut. You're just a... you're just a normal human.

I knot my hands behind her back and press my face into her shoulder. I breathe her in. We should probably go back to Lizzie's house. We should probably call Skye's dad, or one of our parents. We should get someone to pick us up. We should go home.

But Niamh's heart is humming in my ear, her hair tickling my cheek. It's dark out here, and there's no one around to see.

I HOPE YOU'RE HAPPY

Ana's phone blew up on the drive home from the hospital. It was on silent mode, but the notifications kept interrupting the navigation. She knew the route well, but she liked being able to see it mapped out in front of her; she liked the soothing voice reminding her what to do. The messages were all from Chloe.

Ana would know they were from Chloe even if her name, followed by several heart emojis, didn't keep popping up on her screen. That morning, before she went in, Ana had messaged Chloe and said she was crying. They didn't do that very often any more, speak about their emotions in a sincere way. Instead, everything was refracted through their history, the events they'd experienced together and separately, side by side. Ana knew Chloe would be concerned. Maybe that was why she said it. But she should have known how quickly Chloe's concern would sour. Ana's cheeks were dry now, her head thumping, eyes burning. She was consumed by a dull, persistent pain, and wondered if that was what Purgatory felt like. Or would feel like, if it was real.

A skinny fox watched her park the car. A witness. She turned off the engine and considered switching her phone off too, letting the messages pile up. They would still be there in the morning. She knew it was sensible to leave it; she should wait to respond. She told herself that's what she would do, but then something overwhelmed her, like a terrible wave. Doing nothing, or even slowing down, no longer seemed an option. Ana opened the messages and started reading. Her heart rattled around in her chest like a pinball. She typed furiously and pressed send, without bothering to read her message back.

It was late. A group of drunk girls screamed with laughter somewhere further down the road. Ana got out of the car quickly to avoid them and let herself into her building. She felt exhausted and nauseous and relieved, like a shard of glass had been removed from her body. The flat was dark – Callum must be asleep – but the curtains were open, the living room carpet striped by light from the street lamps outside. Ana checked her messages. Three dots appeared inside a speech bubble. They rippled and flickered, over and over, trippy traffic lights in greyscale. What would Chloe say next? There was something strangely thrilling about it: waiting to see how Chloe would twist the knife this time, wondering how much it would hurt, whether they could recover.

The first time, it came as a shock to realize Chloe could so easily withdraw contact. Ana couldn't eat. It was the most acute grief she had ever felt. When they eventually reconciled, Callum commented on the lift in her mood, the way she lit up whenever Chloe messaged. But what had it cost? With a spike of shame, Ana remembered the cookie she'd sent, the word 'SORRY' piped in blue icing. She thought about the person who received the order and had to make that cookie, her pitiful apology squeezed out of their icing pen. She couldn't do that again. She wouldn't.

Without warning, the dots disappeared. They didn't slow down or fade out. They left no mark. They simply vanished. Ana stared at her phone, her own message a tsunami of blue, dominating the screen. She started to type something else, but the little blue arrow beside her message turned green, which meant Chloe's phone had been switched off, run out of battery or lost signal. Or, more likely, Ana had been blocked again. She threw her phone across the room. It landed on the carpet with a soft thud. There was more she needed to say, stuck deep inside her. She needed Chloe to respond in order to dislodge it. Ana grabbed a cushion from the sofa and considered screaming into it, but the gesture felt too dramatic. She thought about writing Chloe an email – she couldn't be blocked on email yet, surely? – but that felt over the top too, unnecessary. It would make her seem deranged. And on reflection, Ana began to feel that perhaps she had been too impulsive, too cruel, her vision blurred by the velocity of her fury. Ana scrolled up to read the message back. *Fuck you, Chloe...* it began. She stopped reading and locked her phone. The photo of her and Callum smiling on holiday in Majorca appeared briefly, then the screen turned black.

Ana sat in the bath and cried. The rush of water from the taps. The lavender- and jasmine-scented bath salts. Her own self-pity thickening around her. She could sense it rising up like tar, slowing things down. She kept checking her phone. Nothing. Nothing. Nothing. Nothing. Green: the colour of life, leaves, green for connection, green for go, green for yes, good, correct, now transformed into green for no. Green for shut out. Blocked. Green for fuck you, too.

The next evening, Ana went out for dinner with a friend from school. Moments after they sat down, Emily announced she was pregnant.

Oh, wow.

It was just the two of them; there was nowhere to hide. Ana was surprised, but she didn't have any reason to be. Emily and her husband had recently bought a place, a little maisonette out towards Twickenham with a patch of patio and dirt that Emily (lovingly, gushingly) called their garden. This was the next logical step. Ana tried to muster up more happiness. Emily was overjoyed, and Ana wanted to be happy for her, but she couldn't. There was an absence where happiness should have been.

Ana tried again.

That's so great.

Her voice came out robotic, empty. She looked up, ready to apologize – *I don't know what's wrong with my voice* – and maybe blame it on the thing with Chloe, her mum,

problems at work, or make up something different altogether, but Emily hadn't even noticed. She was too busy
scouring the menu for something that didn't contain any
alcohol, caffeine, cured meats, soft cheese or refined sugar.

Ana placed the closed menu on the table in front of her.
She would order the steak. Medium rare, peppercorn sauce.
She picked up her phone and swiped through the apps on
a loop – news, people's faces, people saying things, things
to buy – until Chloe appeared. All the blood in Ana's body
rushed in the wrong direction, like a sand timer turned on its
head. Chloe was smiling, relaxed, like she didn't have a care
in the world. The photo had been shared by one of Chloe's
friends from work. They were out for dinner too. There was
more than one photo. Ana swiped through them: Chloe
laughing, Chloe eating, Chloe raising a glass of wine, a selfie
of Chloe and the other friend in some kind of auditorium.
Maybe at a cinema or a theatre, it was hard to tell.

Are you ready to order?

Ana looked up. Emily was smiling at her. The waiter
was waiting. A bright pink cocktail had appeared in front
of her. It had a blue umbrella stuck in the top. Ana ordered
the steak and took a sip of her cocktail. It tasted like jelly
beans.

On the way home, Ana popped into Boots at the station. She picked up a new skincare product and she thought
about calling Chloe. She heard a song on the radio by an
artist they liked, and she thought about texting Chloe. She
opened her book, and the main character was Chloe. She
watched a television show about women living together in

a city, and there she was. Chloe. Dancing around in her underwear to songs by Busted and Destiny's Child, letting Ana sleep in her bed whenever they were sad, because they were always sad together, never alone. Chloe wrote little Post-it notes and stuck them to the fridge before job interviews, or when Ana had to visit her mother: *you got this, you are the best, I love you 4eva.*

·   ·   ·

Soon, it was Ana's birthday. Callum wanted her to go out and have some fun, but she refused. She stayed sprawled on the sofa, drinking home-made margaritas and scrolling through Chloe's social media profiles. Had she been expecting a gesture of reconciliation today because it was her birthday? Perhaps, but it wasn't only Chloe. Emily messaged, but only to see if Ana could go shopping with her on the weekend for baby things, so clearly she had forgotten. Ana's mother sent a message at around midday: *Did my card arrive???* Which meant that she, too, had forgotten but wasn't going to admit it and would instead blame the incompetence of the postal service. Ana didn't respond. She received a card from her sister which simply said *Dear Ana, Happy Birthday – have a great day! Love Lina and Josh.* It was such a generic, impersonal message that Ana wished they hadn't bothered sending anything at all. Was she the kind of person who didn't get one single meaningful card on her birthday? Was that who she had become? There was Callum, of course. Callum had written her a sweet card and made her favourite dinner. Ana knew she should be grateful, but it was too much to expect one person to be everything. The thought made her feel suffocated – though she knew it was *she* who was being suffocating – and she spent long stretches of time thinking about breaking up with him so he could be free of the burden of whatever it was about her that everyone else hated so much.

Ana's thumb hovered over Chloe's face-in-miniature at the top of her feed, wrapped in the cheerful pink-and-yellow circle that meant she had something to show off about. There was a full post on her timeline at least once a week these days, even though she had once said it was narcissistic to post that often. At first, Ana thought the incessant attention-seeking showed that Chloe wasn't happy, that she was trying to make herself feel better with the validation of likes, but now she didn't know. She'd thumbed through the grid a hundred times: Chloe by the river in a brightly coloured jumpsuit and dark sunglasses, holding two Aperol spritzes; photos Chloe had taken of a 'breathtaking' immersive exhibition at an art gallery off the Strand; Chloe's feet in sparkling sand, her toenails perfectly pink, clear seawater rushing over them again and again and again on an infinite loop. Chloe's life captured in neat, beautiful squares. When she saw Chloe's face now, Ana no longer felt like she had been thumped in the stomach. There was still a shard of something, a hot scratch of jealousy or shame, but the overarching feeling was one of sombre acceptance. Ana hesitated, her thumb poised above Chloe's face. She wanted to see what Chloe was up to, but it was impossible. She couldn't bear the thought of Chloe knowing that she had watched the story. She would know it was Ana's birthday. Chloe would not have forgotten.

She's just trying to make you jealous, Callum said.

Oh. Ana looked up, momentarily disoriented.

You know that's why she's posting so much, right? That's why she hasn't blocked you on any of her social media profiles. She wants you to know how much fun she's having. Try not to let it get to you.

I'm not. It's fine.

But every time she opened the apps, Chloe was there. Her face, her life, all of it there, staring back at her. But of course it was. Ana was feeding the algorithm, wasn't she? She offered it the hours she spent looking at Chloe's face, trying to read her posture and the lines around her eyes; the humiliation she felt every time she typed Chloe's username into the search bar. Not using the apps wasn't an option. What else would she do with all the time she had now? Bags and bags of it, her days sagging and empty where she used to be in contact with Chloe. She missed all that now, the constant communication, even though at times she thought it was a bit much. Annoying, even. She had complained to Callum: Why won't she leave me alone for five minutes? But now, well. Things had changed.

I wish there was something I could do, Callum said.

Ana looked into his face: his lined forehead, eyes glimmering with anguish. He was trying to be kind, trying to help. He wanted to understand.

It's okay. Let's just not…

Callum shrugged. Ana closed her eyes. Her head

throbbed. Just then, her phone began vibrating on the coffee table. The screen lit up with an incoming call from her mother. Ana and Callum both watched the screen flashing until the call rang out and the screen went dark again.

Ana thought about reaching out. Even started to type mes-sages sometimes, before remembering that the words would be eaten by the network.

So I guess you're not ready to talk yet...

So I guess we should talk...

I'd really like to talk...

Can we talk?

This is so stupid. You are such a bad friend. Would you just think of someone else, other than yourself, for once in your stupid fucking life?

. . .

Ana met up with Emily outside a huge shopping centre in West London. She got the Tube and Emily drove her new SUV, which she and her husband had selected after taking into consideration the car's environmental credentials, safety rating and boot space. They had been to test drive a few and they'd put together a spreadsheet to compare them all. Ana listened while they stood on the escalator and thought about how much easier it was to order things online. She hated the luminous, clinical feel of the mall, all those white floors and shiny escalators whirring past each other. It felt like being inside a state-of-the-art machine.

She didn't like the aimless walking. She didn't like the endless searching for something unspecific – something she wouldn't know she wanted until she saw it – when it was much easier to simply wait at home for the desire to arise and order the item instantly from her phone.

We've bought the car seat already, Emily said. And the ISOFIX base. You have to buy those things new.

Ana nodded. The sun was dazzling through the glass ceiling. It was warm outside, but inside was so well air-conditioned that the hairs on her arms were standing on end. She gripped the handrail while Emily continued speaking.

I want to pick up some of the smaller bits today. You know, muslins, blankets. Maybe some clothes… The cute things.

Ana nodded again. She rubbed her eye. It stung. She must have got moisturizer in it somehow. She blinked several times, then turned to Emily and smiled.

They spent hours pondering outfits. Rows of dungarees and tiny frilled jackets. Vests emblazoned with words like DADDY'S DARLING, FUTURE CEO and FOREVER HAPPY. Stacks of perfectly pressed suits for sleeping. Blankets rolled up like sushi and tied with a bow. Ana went through the motions, nodding and cooing and clapping when required, but inside her nothing was happening. When Emily disappeared inside a changing room or a toilet cubicle, she marvelled at the ridiculousness of it all. How had she ended up here? Had she, at some point, mistakenly given the impression that this was something she was interested in – babies and their accoutrements? Was it her duty, as a friend, to pretend to be interested? Was everyone doing this, every day, pretending to be interested in things that did not interest them for the sake of their relationships? It was possible she was the only one who objected to this, and the thought made her feel petulant and burdensome.

In the cafe afterwards, over strawberry milkshakes, Emily showed Ana a photo from her most recent scan. Ana took the phone from Emily's hand and zoomed in on the baby's head, a staticky cloud of white. There was a new person growing inside her friend, a fully formed person with a brain and a heart, fleshing out inside her friend's body as they sat there sucking synthetic ice cream through a straw. It was miraculous. It was magic. So why didn't she feel anything?

Ana was invited to marvel at the new car and be driven home, but she declined. She lived on the other side of town, and besides, Emily needed to get home and rest. Emily insisted that she was fine and that she'd like to, but Ana insisted back and eventually she won. On the Tube, she put on her headphones and looked at all the grime-stained seats, the floor streaked with mud and crumbs, a nest of hair and fluff. Opposite, a couple sat on the faded seats, their baby in a pram beside them. Ana couldn't see the baby, but she could hear it grunting and see little white-clad feet kicking up into the air. The parents weren't paying attention. They were looking at something on one of their phones. They were laughing. The man, who had a soft, bespectacled face and a wave of greying hair, squeezed the woman's thigh and dropped a kiss on top of her head. The woman was blondish, the darker roots of her hair spreading down past her ears, so grown out it almost looked like the position of the dye was intentional, just a bad balayage, but the sharp delineation of colour gave it away. They looked tired but content, the fine lines on their faces picked out by the fluorescent overhead lighting. But – the baby. The grunts turned into cries, and Ana turned up her headphones. She looked the other way as the couple shared a kiss. The Tube carriage rattled and shrieked. The baby was wailing now, and she wasn't the only passenger who had noticed. Other people were looking around now, wondering but not asking if anyone was going to pick up the baby. Eventually the woman scowled and rattled the pram's handle.

Shush, she said. Go to sleep now.

The baby's cries became more mournful, warbling, its little voice shuddering and shaking. Ana gripped the pole in front of her and turned her music off and back on again, louder this time. She couldn't bear to listen, but at the same time it felt awful, wrong, to ignore the baby. But what could she do? It wasn't a crime to let your baby cry, was it? Lots of people let their babies cry, and they were all fine. Well, most of them anyway. Ana thought about what it would be like to be so small and helpless and on a Tube carriage like this: the strange sounds, the strange smells, not knowing where your familiar humans had gone, feeling small and alone. She tried to stop, to think about something else, anything else. Beaches. Sunshine. Christmas. She imagined herself snapping, losing control and screaming across the carriage: *Just pick up your fucking baby.* Her breath caught in her chest. It felt like the walls of the carriage were folding in on her. She closed her eyes. The train clattered into a station and the doors whooshed open. The couple stood up and Ana watched as the man took hold of the pram's handle and manoeuvred it through the sliding doors and onto the platform without once looking down at the baby. Its cries were quieter now, whimpers, lost to the roar of station sounds. People getting on, people getting off, someone asking for some change so they could get a room at a hostel tonight, someone else asking urgently *Does this train go to Edgware? Well, does it?*

. . .

Ana learned of her own pregnancy slowly. She thought it would come to her in a flash of realization, the way it did in movies. She thought it would be obvious from her dry-heaving over the toilet first thing in the morning or falling asleep in the middle of the day. Instead, it was a slow, creeping process, like waiting for an answer to emerge from the purple liquid of a Magic 8 ball, an answer like BETTER NOT TELL YOU NOW, or SIGNS POINT TO YES. One day, on the way to work, she went to a Sainsbury's Local and looked at the pregnancy tests on the shelves. The branded tests that had started to pop up on her social media – Clearblue, First Response – packed in alongside the supermarket own-brand tests, all waiting in their neat, vaguely medical packaging, waiting with their answers. She left without buying one, telling herself her period would arrive later that day, or the next. It didn't.

She thought about telling Callum. But she knew she wouldn't be able to answer his questions. Why not go for it? he would ask her. What was wrong with them, now, their life? Hadn't she always said she was open to it, wanted it one day, even? Why not now? And anyway, what else was she going to do? It wasn't like she loved her job, sitting on reception all day, booking out meeting rooms and ordering catering for client lunches. It wasn't like she had a career to think about. And she could take maternity leave. Think of all that time off! Perhaps they could move out of London, like they'd always talked about, to somewhere with more space. Get a dog, maybe. He would run with it. He would take it out of her hands. He would insist that this was for the best; that this would make them happy.

Ana wasn't bloated, her breasts didn't ache. She woke up feeling like she had a mild hangover most days, but that might have been due to the fact that she was still drinking most evenings. Why should she stop? It was frustrating to have to take time to sort out something that wasn't affecting her day-to-day life much at all, but she knew it wouldn't be long until it did. Ana thought of those images of pregnancy tissue, soft clouds in Petri dishes. She knew it wasn't a big deal. It was her body, her right. A right she was grateful to have. She thought of all the pro-choice protesters with their placards raised high. She read the information on the NHS website: *You may want to speak to your partner, friends or family, but you do not have to.*

They do not have a say in your decision. It was validating, in a way.

On the day of the abortion, Ana took the bus to the clinic. She stared out of the window at the dull November day, everything washed in grey. She passed hundreds of people. All of them seemed to be slightly damp. When she got off the bus, she felt shaky, which was probably travel sickness – buses always made her feel like that. The last time she had been to an abortion clinic she was seventeen. They were there for Chloe's abortion. Ana usually thought of this incident as an example of what a great friend she was. She had booked the appointment for Chloe, taken her to the clinic and waited with a can of Coke and a pack of maxi pads. Now, entering a similar but different clinic, she remembered different details. The waiting room, with its pale, cornflower-blue walls and scratchy grey carpet; the way she sat with her arms folded, stony-faced. Chloe wouldn't tell Ana who had got her pregnant, and Ana was cross: she felt it was her right to know. Maybe she could have been a more supportive friend, but at the same time she was only seventeen. She was still a child. They both were. But they were in touching distance of thirty now, and where was Chloe? Even if Ana had wanted her here, Chloe could never have known. She wasn't around to return the favour.

When she was called in for her scan, the nurse confirmed that Ana was about seven weeks pregnant. The room was bright and high up, blinds open. The spindly fingers of leaf-less trees stretched into the vast white expanse of sky.

Would you like to see? the nurse asked her in a low, understanding voice.

Ana looked away and shook her head. She accepted a stack of blue towels to wipe the jelly off her stomach. The nurse handed her a file and told her to give it in at the reception desk. On the way down the corridor, Ana found herself walking off to the side, towards the toilets. She locked herself in the cubicle and opened the file. Inside, a small, glossy black-and-white image. She looked at it closely. There it was: the mysterious inner workings of her body. A cavernous black space and a tiny white blob in the middle. Ana thought of the image Emily had shown her over milkshakes. The blob that looked like a baby, a whole future contained within it. Almost the diametrical opposite of this blob. Ana slipped the image back into the file, left the cubicle and handed it in at the reception desk, just as she'd been told to.

Suddenly, everyone was pregnant. At work, three people: two account managers and one senior client manager. The younger ones came into the office with their BABY ON BOARD badges and waited to be congratulated. The client manager had been pregnant for a while, apparently, but Ana had missed the announcement. She saw her in the glass lift opposite the reception desk, caressing the tight globe of her belly straining out of her suit. Ana thought of the sea witch from Disney's *The Little Mermaid*, the way she burst out of her human body, the clothes torn and shredded, when she transformed into a monster. Nicole, who worked alongside Ana on reception, was constantly monitoring the female members of the team, assessing their clothes, the shapes of their waists. Nicole knew all the gossip; she would be the first to know. Ana shifted in her maxi pad, heard it crinkle and crease against her leggings.

The first few days, the blood was heavier than she'd ever known. She didn't know how much was too much. She just had to wait and hope. Sometimes, she fished through the dark clots on her pad; some were solid, some jellylike, some burst into liquid when she poked them. She wasn't looking for anything in particular, but she was intrigued by the mechanics of her body, all this *stuff* she'd created without even knowing it, without even trying. When she was in the bath, it bloomed out of her, a rusty cloud in the water.

Emily texted a few times. Once she even called, which was unlike her. Ana didn't respond. It seemed disingenuous somehow to meet up and not talk about the abortion. But at the same time, she didn't see how they could talk about it. They were each caught up in their incompatible experiences. There was a line drawn, and Ana didn't know how to cross it. She imagined how it would go. Emily would falter. She wouldn't be able to hide her disappointment. Or worse still, her sorrow. She might even cry. No, it was better to leave her out of it. Ana decided to cut Chloe out too, for good, a choice Nicole enthusiastically supported. Ana blocked her across all methods of communication – WhatsApp, Instagram, iMessage, email – all of it. It wasn't that she thought Chloe would get in touch after all this time had passed, but more that she wanted to impose a conclusion on their friendship, one Chloe had kept from her. It felt good to wipe her out, like an annoying blot on a white jumper that finally washes clean.

Ana spent more of her evenings at home with Callum, watching Netflix and eating dinner on the sofa. On weekends, they cleaned their flat from top to bottom while they each listened to their separate podcasts. They talked about places they could go on holiday: things they might do, food they might try. They visited local markets to buy Christmas presents, or they went for long, chilly walks around the park and to the pub for a roast dinner. At night, they sat in bed side by side, reading their books. Ana was relieved to learn that she could still have her secrets; that she could keep a small part back, just for herself.

·   ·   ·

One night, Ana's phone rang. Lina's face flashed up on the screen, lighting the dark bedroom like a siren. Ana wasn't surprised. She knew what was coming; this was overdue. On the other end of the line, Lina's voice sounded broken, almost primal in her rage. She shouted that she couldn't take it any longer, that she was sick of taking up all the slack. She called Ana self-involved, a coward and a bitch, among other things. These words must have hurt once, but Ana felt nothing now. They slid off her as though she was watching a television show, or listening to some other sisters on the street, people she didn't know. Callum wanted to come with her, said he'd drive, but Ana refused. She wasn't protecting her mother or sister from his judgement, but if there were fewer people involved, it was easier to take control. The narrative, the memories, herself – everything could be mastered.

Lina was on the walkway outside their mother's front door. She was pacing up and down and she was smoking, which didn't suit her. She looked like a little girl playing at being an adult. The lights were on, but there were no noises coming from inside the flat. Perhaps their mother was asleep. Motorbikes roared and spluttered in the distance. The light was cold and blue. Lina looked up. She was surprised. Perhaps she hadn't believed Ana would come at all.

You did this, she said. I hope you're happy now.

Her voice was low and cutting. She threw her cigarette butt over the balcony edge. Ana watched as it fell down, down, down to the ground, like a fallen star, a tiny meteor.

Inside, the flat was a mess. Drawers had been upturned: ribbons, receipts, clothes, cutlery, food, all scattered across the floor. Their mother had been looking for something. Ana wondered whether she had hurtled around the room screaming or emptied the drawers methodically with a careful, trance-like precision. She was never sure which was worse. The shouting was most immediately distressing, but at least then her mother's pain was intelligible.

Lina shook out a bin bag and started to search through the jumble of things on the floor. She used her foot to push objects aside, looking for whatever was broken and needed to be thrown away. After a while, she spoke.

I'm sorry, okay? I shouldn't have said all that stuff.

It's fine, Ana said. You don't need to be sorry. I'm sorry.

It's not your fault.

It's not your fault either.

Ana lifted a crumpled shirt from the sofa and folded it. The truth is that it was no one's fault. It was just one of those things, but that didn't make it hurt any less. For years, Ana had had so much anger towards their mother, unable to fathom why she couldn't remember to take the medication. It had all seemed so simple then, as though drugs could be an answer, a final fix for anything.

What caused it this time?

Oh. Lina looked up. Um, I think the water was off. A burst pipe on the main road.

Ana nodded. She could imagine how that would have gone down.

Is it back on now?

Lina went over to the kitchen and ran the tap. Water spluttered out weakly.

Kinda?

At least that's something.

Yeah. Look at this.

Lina held out a small object towards Ana. It was a fridge magnet. The three of them on a roller coaster at Chessington World of Adventures. Ana must have been about thirteen – she was wearing her secondary school tie – and Lina was still in her primary school uniform: a purple jumper and a white polo shirt. Their mother's arms were in the air, an outsized grin plastered onto her face. The two sisters were smiling politely, enjoying their truancy while they could.

Aw, Ana said. You were cute back then.

I'm still cute now.

Ana snorted. Okay, sure.

Hey!

They looked at each other and instinctively looked away.

So long ago now.

Yep. Time flies and all that.

It really does.

Their mother hadn't been well that day, but they didn't know it yet. Driving way too fast and singing along to the radio, her eyes wild. Ana couldn't listen to 'Burning Up' any more without reliving the giddy sense of possibility she'd felt when their mother announced that they were skipping school. That, and the end of the day, when she had slapped Lina across the face for vomiting on herself, streaks of bright pink and blue from all the candyfloss and sweets. Ana thought about asking Lina if she remembered that bit too, but maybe she had forgotten. What a gift that would be. What would be the point in reminding her now?

Before long, the flat was tidy. Everything was back where it belonged, as though time had been wound back.

You should go home, Ana said.

No, it's fine, Lina said. You can go home. I'll stay.

But I've hardly done anything.

Okay, so it'll be your turn next.

Seriously. You should sleep.

I just... I want to stay. I want to be here when she wakes up.

Ana looked at her sister, folded into herself on the sofa. Lina's eyes were raw but bright. She wasn't crying. She was looking closely at her phone and blinking hard, probably texting Josh. Ana wanted to say something – something reassuring or kind, something to make the situation better. But anything that could be said had been said many times before.

I'll come back first thing in the morning.

. . .

When the baby was born, Emily invited Ana to visit. It had been almost four months since they'd last seen each other, a period of time that felt at once short and impossibly long. Long enough for a foetus to grow from the size of a grape-fruit to the size of a newborn baby; for the baby's lungs to grow strong enough to breathe outside her mother's body. Long enough for Ana's mother to be back to her version of normal. For now at least. On the train journey, Ana turned her music up loud and stared out of the window at the sky, lit up with golden-blue winter sunshine. The face of a child about two years old appeared in the gap between the seats in front of her. The child stuck out her tongue and wiggled her head. Ana removed her headphones and stuck out her own tongue in response. The child giggled, and Ana felt as though she had been struck by sunlight. She thought about the cells that could have been her own child. There was a residual sadness there, a crack of pain, the pain that came with the end of anything. It was the same thing she felt when she thought about Chloe these days: a feeling of longing but also of acceptance. There were many things in a person's life that couldn't be changed, but there were also many things that could. It was a comforting thought: her life was one of random chance and of her own construction. Soon, Ana would arrive at Emily's house, and she would hold the baby. The baby's eyes would be open, both wise and unseeing, her face full of possibility and a terrifying vulnerability that made Ana's tummy flip. Ana would be overwhelmed by both love and the certainty that she would never have children of her own. She couldn't. She wouldn't. But that was all right. Other things would come.

Cowboy/Superhero/
Spaceman/Monster

Sunday, last show of the week. I am stationed in the basement. There is nothing to see except creeping fog, which hisses on at timed intervals, and a distant crack of light. When I look down, I can barely see my hands splayed in front of me. The soundtrack crescendoes, a static rumbling that makes my chest ache. The first ushering shift I ever did was in the basement. I remember the cold, drenching fear, the kind I have only felt once before, when I was mugged at knifepoint on my way home from school. My heart was roaring so loud I could hear nothing else, and my body went limp, given over to my impending death. I was thinking crazy things – the job was some sort of elaborate trick, I was about to be ritually sacrificed to some weird cult. But eventually the audience trickled down, as they always do, and the space filled with the white-masked faces of other humans.

Another figure dressed all in black appears at the end of the corridor. A fellow usher, or a member of the stage management team. I check my watch. We aren't due to change positions for another twenty-five minutes.

Fancy that, a voice says, close to my ear. Finding you down here all alone.

It's The Friend. I catch my left wrist in my right hand behind my back and hold it tight. I feel my pulse jumping like something small and frightened is trying to escape.

Fancy that, I say. Looking up my location on the rota... Are you stalking me?

He smirks. I can only see pale lips and a chin speckled with dun-coloured stubble. The black mask covers the top half of his face.

Aren't you good, staying where you're supposed to be.

And where exactly are you supposed to be?

In the desert.

You're missing the naked cowboy just for me?

The desert is on the top floor, another floor that usually remains empty until the second hour of the performance. There was a whole drama with the desert before the show opened. There weren't enough bags of sand, and there was a big question mark over how long the horse could stay up there without needing a break. His name is Chestnut, and he goes up and down in the lift about three times a day. In between shows, the Head of Animal Handling takes him for a canter in Hyde Park.

Nah, the naked cowboy's bit isn't for another ten minutes. I don't like you enough to miss out on that.

Ha, I say into the dark. So you *do* like me.

Keep up, little one.

The Friend leans closer. The music crashes into wailing strings – a track from a horror movie. The innocent girl, alone, making her way through the creepy house. I can smell the cigarettes and coffee on his breath, the minty freshness of his shower gel, and something musky and animalic which could be sex or shit.

I know you like me too, he says. Just admit it.

Nah. This is a one-way thing, I say. You're the one stalking me, three floors down from where you're supposed to be.

Stop playing hard to get, he says. He grabs hold of my wrist then lets it go. Think of all the fun we could have if you admitted that you want me.

I applied for the job on a whim. At the time, I was sending out applications indiscriminately, wanting to do something – anything – else with my days. I was sick of stacking shelves at the supermarket across the road from my flat. I spent my days off at the same supermarket with The Boyfriend. My basket would be full of tins, frozen ready meals, and as a treat a little bottle of supermarket own-brand vodka. His would be full of fruit, cakes, fresh bread, wine, butter. He was buying the food for me, and we both knew it, but we had to pretend otherwise. He liked the performance, the suspense, the anticipation of his departure when I would say *Don't forget your food shopping* and he would say *That's not my food, I bought it for you*, and I would gush with gratitude and he would act like it was no big deal, which I suppose maybe it wasn't. For him.

I was ready for a change. The ad said the show was immersive. A site-specific theatre dance experience. I didn't know what that meant at the time, not being the theatre type, but I thought it sounded promising. More fun than stacking loo rolls anyway. I called my mum when I got the job, and she asked me if I was sure it wasn't a sex thing. Lots of people just don't get it. Aside from the fans in the Facebook group – the Superfans, who visit again and again – most audience members miss out one or two floors entirely on their first visit. I'd had complaints about it when I worked cover shifts in the box office:

But I didn't even get to see the whole show! My friend saw this orgy in the basement. I didn't even get to the basement.

That's the point, I'd reply. It's literally impossible to see everything. You have to make choices.

This is ridiculous, they'd huff. How can I choose when I don't know what I'm choosing *from*?

I'd shrug. I was only a box office assistant. What did I care?

You're welcome to return and try again, I'd say. We have availability from mid-October.

My favourite complaints of all were from people who missed the show completely, having got their dates mixed up. They always demanded a refund; righteously, as though it was somehow my fault and not their own stupidity.

But we didn't get to see the show at all! they'd say.

I'm sorry, I'd say. But that's like trying to return an item of clothing that no longer exists.

But we didn't see the show!

I was a bit antagonistic, sure, but it was one of the perks of the job, getting to wind rich people up. Sometimes the women cried, their eyes clouding over with the impossible unfairness of it all. But I remained strong. It was my job, I reminded them. My hands were tied. They always paid up in the end. They could swallow the cost no problem. It was all an act designed to elicit sympathy, and I never fell for it. Sometimes I refunded their orders anyway, after they had paid for new tickets, and pocketed the cash.

We were told the audience would be mostly made up of two categories of people: the Tourists and the Good Timers. They just wanted to have fun. All we had to do was facilitate their good time within the rules of the world.

Imagine a Good Timer comes up to you, and they're frustrated because they can't find the bar. What do you do? Karina?

This was at our induction workshop. We were in a large, draughty room, which must have been an old office. The carpet was grey and rough and covered in worn black wads of chewing gum. We sat on stools in a circle almost as wide as the room. Everyone's eyes were on Karina.

Um, she said. So, we're not allowed to speak?

Not unless it's an emergency.

Can I ask them if it's an emergency?

The facilitator of the induction workshop, who I've not seen since, looked around the room, his eyes alight with glee. Wrong answer, he said.

Anyone else?

I can't remember what the right answer was now. I was getting bored. But in a nutshell, we were told to hold the Superfans at arm's length, call the police on the Obsessives and pander to the Tourists and the Good Timers as much as we could. We weren't given much direction on how to deal with the Young Creatives, probably because most of us belonged in that category and any sense that we were being 'handled' would have compromised the illusion.

Every production has its roles, the facilitator said as we left the room. Don't forget how to play yours.

· · ·

When the show finishes and the lights go up, the place looks less ominous. There are thirty or so of us in the ice palace, sitting on the black linoleum floor, surrounded by glittering glaciers of white and blue. A member of the stage management crew is testing out the trapeze, swinging through the air above our heads. There are boxes and boxes of masks; not the black ones we wear, but the white ones the audience wear, with gaping eyeholes and pointed mouths, not unlike the mask from Scream. We clean each one with a disinfectant wipe. Usually this is straightforward, but sometimes we find the imprint of someone's face inside – lipstick, mascara, foundation, blusher – which is both terrifying and disgusting in equal measure. One time a mask was full of tiny snippings of hair.

The front-of-house manager, The Boss, stands in front of us and clears his throat. He is a little man, not much taller than me, with floppy white hair that curls past his shoulders. He wears combat boots and speaks the way he walks: slowly, ploddingly.

Howdy everyone, he says. Howdy. It was an eventful show tonight. We had to ask one audience member to leave, which was a pity, but he was following Kirsty way too close. You might have seen him before – he's an Obsessive. I think he has a 'thing' for her, but he started to get aggressive tonight and yeah, that was it! Had to go. Kirsty's fine, but let's be vigilant going forward, yeah? He's not allowed back in again. Sally?

The assistant front-of-house manager steps forward. No one likes her much. She has a laugh like a hyena.

Hi, hi. Just a quick reminder from me that you're not here to watch the show… unfortunately! I know, I know. So please stay in your allocated position, all right? If I come to check on you and I can't see you anywhere in the vicinity of where you're supposed to be… well, that's a problem. Also, not to nag, but can we please stay on the correct radio channel? I need to be able to get in contact with you if something happens. If I can't, then you may as well not be here. Sorry to be blunt.

Sally shifts from foot to foot and wipes her nose with the cuff of her black fleece.

What else… What else. Oh! We had a few panic attacks in the audience tonight. Thank you to Lucy and Siobhan for dealing so well with those. An injury too. Someone fell off the stage on the first floor, you know, where the movie set is? By the high school locker room? Anyway, I think his leg's broken. He had to go off in an ambulance, so let's make sure audience members don't climb up there in future.

Ouch, says The Boss. Sounds rough.

Sally shrugs and makes a strange expression, sympathetic but also mean, as though she thinks the guy with the broken leg got what he deserved. I think of him being pulled out of the show and into an ambulance, not by NHS paramedics in their neat, green uniforms but by The Doctor from the show, with his crooked bow tie, his slicked-down centre parting and his white coat. I've seen him take individual audience members into his little room on the first floor, the walls covered in Rorschach inkblots and Snellen eyesight charts. On the shelves, a skull and a hovering eye, complete with stem, preserved in some kind of liquid.

The Boss and Sally look at each other, and for a split second I think they're going to kiss.

All right, so there's some money behind the bar tonight, Sally says. From production. To say thanks, I suppose. These last few weeks have been difficult, and you've all done a great job. Only one drink each though! This is a trust system, and if you have more than one, you'll be taking a drink from one of your co-workers. That isn't very nice. Okay, so have fun. See you all tomorrow.

The show lives in a huge red-brick building next to the station. It used to be a postal sorting and delivery office, but it's been empty for a few years. Developers are waiting for permission from the council to expand the building into a multifunctional retail, restaurant and office complex

COWBOY/SUPERHERO/SPACEMAN/MONSTER · 171

made almost completely of glass. In the meantime, the production company has been allowed to run the show for an indefinite period of time. The backstage area on the top floor is the only place that hints at the building's former identity. The old cubbyholes remain, along with a few signs bearing London postcode districts. New rooms have been created with temporary walls, flimsy bits of material that don't reach the high ceilings and feel as though they will collapse if you lean on them by accident. The area designated for front-of-house staff is divided into three sections: one for M, one for F, and one general area where we sit around pre- and post-shift talking and eating.

I look at everyone huddled together under the strip lights, untangling their radios, eating bananas, sharing lip balm, and I feel repulsed. I grab a packet of cigarettes out of my jacket pocket and cross the top floor, past clots of people dissecting that night's show, performers peeling off their wigs, someone extricating themselves from a scarlet feather boa, and climb out of a low window onto the roof. It is basement-dark. As my eyes adjust, I look out at the BT Tower glowing in the distance. My mum told me there used to be a spinning restaurant up there, but I don't know if I believe her. It doesn't seem likely that people would want to spin round and round while they ate their dinner.

Hello, a voice says.

Hi.

It isn't The Friend this time. I can't make out who it is, only a shadowy shape and an orange pinprick of light.

So, tell me what you do.

The voice is smooth and authoritative and sounds like it belongs to someone much older than me. I move closer. It is one of the performers. He sits cross-legged, head resting against the metal railings. I think of the long, empty space between his head and the pavement several floors below, and my tummy plummets. He is wearing some kind of fur hat, which looks like a dead animal on his head. It is August. He must be very hot.

I'm an usher, I say. Box office too, sometimes.

But what do you *do*?

I squint into the darkness. Nothing really, I say, and instantly regret it. Everybody else has something. Nearly all the other ushers are creatives of some kind: actors, dancers, writers, filmmakers. They work here to support their creative endeavours. But not me. I get asked that question a lot in this building: what I do. At first, I didn't understand why gesturing around and saying 'this' was not a satisfactory answer. The Hat takes a thoughtful drag of his roll-up, although by now it is practically burning his fingers, smoked right down to the filter. The silence makes me feel uncomfortable, so I try to think of something funny and ironic to say about his headwear. Before I can come up with anything, he flicks his butt off the roof and speaks again.

Sometimes doing nothing is the most difficult thing of all.

Right, I say. Right... But you're an actor. Isn't that harder than doing nothing? Like, staying in character, remembering lines... Didn't you have to do training and stuff, a degree?

He smiles, a dreamy, distant expression, and turns towards the window. More people are scrambling through. We sit for a while and listen to their conversations, their stupid laughter.

.   .   .

The Boyfriend and I aren't getting along. After one argument, I threw his guitar at the wall. I don't know what it was doing in my flat. It didn't break, which was amazing really. Another time I dropped his iPhone from my bedroom window, and it shattered into a million pieces. Some of the glass turned to dust. I watched as he went down and picked up the device from the tarmac. He brought it back and showed me the missing chunks, gaping holes that revealed the phone's internal organs. He wanted to claim it on insurance, but they wouldn't go for it. It was clear it had been intentionally damaged. He told me I would have to save up to pay him back for his new phone, but he earns three times more than me and it didn't seem fair. So I didn't.

But you *broke* my *phone*, he said, again and again. You threw it out of the *window*.

Yeah, yeah, I thought. But on the outside, I stayed silent. I made sure I looked sorry.

He asks me a lot about the people I work with, especially the performers. I get a train to work now, so he can't stop by the way he used to when I was at the supermarket. If he wanted to surprise me now, he'd need a ticket. When I am out drinking, he requires a full list of everyone present. If there is someone on the list whose name I don't know, like

Some Guy Who Seems to Be Friends with Danny, he makes me ask their name so he can look them up on social media. This is supposed to be a punishment, something to embarrass me. But after the first few times, I start to enjoy it. People are amused to be approached by me. They touch my waist and lean close to hear me speak over the music. Sometimes I get so close I can feel the heat pulse from someone's neck, and my insides quiver. I had my first kiss with a girl this way. She was a dancer called Astrid, a friend of one of the performers. Her hair was long and red and went all the way down to her waist. She told me she'd once been in *Vogue Italia*. Her lips were soft and the air outside was cold and clear like bottled water from a fridge, and for the three minutes we kissed, I didn't think about The Boyfriend once.

.   .   .

I'm signing myself out at the stage door when The Friend from the basement reappears.

It's all right, he says. I haven't left yet.

I roll my eyes and continue writing my name. How was The Cowboy? I ask.

Excellent, as always.

When I move towards the door, he grabs my hand. Not my wrist this time – my hand. His hands are rough, and I realize mine are sweaty. I slide my hand out of his grip.

I'm going home, I say. You're too late.

That's a shame. I thought you were coming for a drink.

I told The Boyfriend I would come straight home. Or rather, he had told me to come straight home after I finished work, and I hadn't said anything in response. We didn't live together but, somehow, he'd ended up with my spare key. I knew he would be waiting for me.

A group of us walk to the Mexican bar down the road. It is the only place that stays open on a Sunday night, so it is where all of us, cast and crew, inevitably end up once the show bar closes. The Mexicans love us. Before the show opened, they had hardly any customers on a Sunday night.

We didn't know why we bothered staying open! the owner yells at me, struggling against the heavy metal pumping over the speakers. But this is why – we knew you were coming! We could feel it in our hearts! You and all of your friends!

I thank him and take a sip of my £5 margarita. My phone buzzes in my pocket with a message from The Boyfriend: *WHERE ARE YOU. IF YOU ARE WITH HIM, I CANNOT BE HELD RESPONSIBLE FOR MY ACTIONS.*

I like the fact he used all caps, the lack of question mark. I take a large sip of my drink. It is so sour it makes my teeth ache. I can see The Friend sat at a table with five other girls – two from wardrobe, two ushers and one of the choreographers. They are all touching each other, trying some playground trick to give each other goosebumps. I briefly wonder if this display is for me, a thought that makes me feel mixed up, at once embarrassed and unbearably sad.

The Hat is already outside, leaning against the wall under a street light. I watch him take one of his little roll-ups out of a dainty silver case.

Why do you wear that thing? I say.

He studies me, cigarette dangling from his lips, unlit. A golden curl of tobacco flutters from the end.

Why do you wear *that* thing? he says in response.

What thing? I look down at my black jeans, my black-and-white striped T-shirt, my plain trainers.

Any of those things.

Because we have to wear clothes?

Why do you wear that skinsuit?

What do you mean?

Your skin, how does it feel when you put it on?

I wonder if The Hat is flirting with me, or if my drink has been spiked. I think about my body, naked, and flinch, fold my arms tight across my chest.

This could be the night I go back to The Hat's flat in Stoke Newington. We snort lines of coke off the screen of his iPad and fuck as the sun rises. Without his hat, he looks like an overgrown baby, lying on his back, helpless. I think I could do anything to him, but that's not true. It's just an illusion. I feel like I am outside my body, watching someone else go through the motions. After a while, it becomes clear he won't come, and so I leave. I step out into the watery daylight and I feel sad, like I have failed, or like something has been taken from me. But deep down I know that anything I've lost has been given away freely.

Or maybe it's the night The Friend appears for a third time, like an apparition, blocking the doorway to the bar as I am about to leave.

Wait, he says. I haven't had a chance to buy you a drink yet.

Oh, you've had your chance, I think but don't say.

Shall we get out of here?

The music starts up then, a blast of brass. He takes my hand and we tip-tap our way to the corner shop. He pops inside and reappears with some little cans of gin and tonic. The journey from Paddington to Camden takes minutes. Our feet barely touch the pavement as we leap and prance and spin, the sky above us smeared with streaks of light pollution, like butter on a car windscreen. He lifts me high above his head at the summit of Primrose Hill and turns slowly in a circle. I hold my body tight together and look out at London, all the lights, all the sights. I feel like I am the BT Tower and there are lots of little people sat inside me looking out and exclaiming *Wow! Would you look at that view?* We collapse on the grass, and he plays the Blur song 'For Tomorrow' on his phone, just for the line about Primrose Hill. We shout the lyrics together, our hands clasped in a knot, swinging up and down in the air like a wrecking ball.

After a while, our backs get cold from the ground. We move to a bench and huddle together, watching the city emerge from the gloom. We wait for sunrise, but it never comes. The sky fades slowly to an off-grey white, the colour of damp, dirty tissues. The Blur song continues to play on repeat, a tinny sound from his pocket. People walk past us with purpose, dressed in their work outfits, their suits and heels, their uniforms, ready for the day to start.

Can you believe people are going to *work*? The Friend says, incredulous, as though the world should have stopped for us.

Yes, I say. Yes, I can.

What do we do after that? We go back to his, I suppose. His tiny, damp bedroom in Stepney Green. We take the Tube, our faces ghastly under the bright lighting. I notice my phone has run out of battery and I think briefly of throwing it away, so The Boyfriend can't ever get in contact with me again.

The Friend lives in a small pebble-dash house just down from the station. There are piles of coins on the top of his chest of drawers and mould speckles one wall. He says the landlord won't do anything about it.

Apparently we just need to open the windows more often.

I nod, like I know. There are several mugs on the floor, half-filled with a grey liquid. The room smells horrible. I lie on top of the clammy duvet and tried not to think about when it was last washed. I allow him to touch me. Why not? We've come this far, haven't we?

I wake at 3 p.m. with the sun blaring through his curtainless window. In the bright light of day, his room is worse than I remembered. I want to scream.

Hey, he says.

Sorry. I should go.

I get dressed and rush out onto the street, light a cigarette, and walk back in the direction of the Tube. I decide I will stop at Primark to buy some new clothes before work. They'll have something black. They always do.

What else, what else? Maybe it is the night I go to see The Doctor and he peers at me closely, taps my forehead with some metal implement and tells me I needed to stop eating so much.

Or else you'll die, he says. I can see burst blood vessels, like red stars in his eyes, his large, oily pores. I nod. I don't want to die.

Maybe it is the night The Cowboy scoops me up from the desert and takes me to a barn dance and his girlfriend, the star of the show, sees us fucking behind the bar.

Maybe I am the star of the show. Maybe I was the star all along.

That afternoon, I go to work, but I don't work. I'm watching the show, I'm in the show. I walk through toyshops and churches, abandoned motel rooms and libraries with polished desks full of paper. I open a drawer and pull out a file. Each sheet of paper has *test test test test test test test test test test* printed all over the page. I throw them up in the air. The Seamstress plucks me out of the darkness, out of the sea of anonymous faces, blank masks, and takes me into her dressing room. I am awestruck by her beauty, the flat roses of her cheeks, those bee-stung lips.

Hi, honey! she says, snapping her gum.

Hi, I say back.

Don't be shy now, she says. I know exactly what to do with you.

She removes my mask and shows me all the dresses she's been working on, swishy and silky, emerald, magenta, glittering gold, poufy, structured, slinky, bejewelled, petticoated.

Wow, I say. I run my fingers along the gowns on the rack and it feels like cool water. It feels refreshing, is what I mean. It feels like something is filling me up.

The Seamstress selects one for me and I put it on. It doesn't matter what it looks like. It fits me perfectly, like a glove. It's gorgeous and comfortable and so lovely that I think I'm going to cry, but The Seamstress stops me.

I'm about to do your make-up, she says. It won't do to have salty streaks down your cheeks now, will it?

I let her take my face into her soft hands. She moves so slowly, so softly, so gently, that I feel like crying again, but I make my mind go blank to stop myself. I imagine a big, white, empty space that I walk around and around, for miles in every direction, and I see nothing and no one. I think, I truly am all alone!

Honey, the Seamstress is saying. Hello, are you still in there?

I'm here.

It's time for you to go.

She's right. I thank her and stand up in my beautiful dress, my painted face. I leave the dressing room and move through the building. All the blank, masked faces watch me, as though I am there for them to look at; as though I have a storyline and a path to follow, the same thing every day on a loop. But I don't.

I walk down the main street with its old-fashioned shop-fronts, past The Cowboy's bar. In the square, I place my hand on the stone fountain, but it isn't solid and hard like I want it to be. I could punch a hole right through it. I make my way down the stairs, masked bodies trailing behind me. I peek into the ice palace. The audience follow my gaze – The Star is lifted high, high into the air; it looks like she'll fall, but The Superhero catches her – and behind them, in the shadows, an usher or a stage manager staring right at me and speaking urgently into a radio. Quicker now. I stride down the corridor, ignoring the staircase that could take me down to the basement or up to the desert. Not this time. I slam open the fire exit, and it's all over. The daylight is blinding. Car fumes and body odour and fried chicken. Beeping horns and barking dogs and someone shouts. This isn't some pretend street with flimsy walls that shudder when slammed. No. This is the real thing. This is something I cannot tear down, no matter how hard I try. I think of my mask, abandoned back in the dressing room. It takes all my willpower not to turn around.

Positive Vibes

First, she laid out the little milk jugs of wildflowers. One on each of the round tables, and three on the long table at the back. Then she laid out the pots of sugar and arranged the croissants and pastries in a glass display cabinet by the till. She put the squashed ones at the back, where they would be selected for sale first, and the best ones up front. Outside, a man knocked on the door and peered through the glass. He was holding a leather laptop bag in his other hand. He tapped his watch and mimed drinking a cup of coffee. Lia shook her head and shrugged apologetically. He gestured for her to come closer, but she stayed where she was. They weren't supposed to open the door to customers unless there were at least two of them in the building. Cora told her it had been company policy ever since there was a robbery-murder at one of the other cafes, over in East London. Lia laughed, but Cora's face remained deadly serious. Later, Lia googled it, but she could find no trace of the murder having actually happened. Still, she made sure the door was double-locked whenever she was on her own.

Cora clattered through the back door; Lia flinched.

Sorry, sorry! Cora called. I didn't sleep well. I'm just gonna get changed, then I'll be right with you.

The cafe's decor was Scandinavian in style, neutral and full of light: blonde wood furniture, blinding white walls. It was March. Spring had finally arrived. Sunlight skittered across the polished tabletops. Outside, yellow and purple crocuses began to poke their heads out of the grass, the sky rinsed clean by the sun. Once she was dressed in the regulation blue jeans, white T-shirt and navy apron, Cora switched on the speakers and upbeat pop pumped out. They were supposed to play music from an approved playlist, which mostly consisted of calming spa-type music, but Cora refused to put it on, even when their boss, Fiona, was in.

I hate it, Cora said. And anyway, this is what people want in the morning, isn't it? A boost! Some fun! I mean, isn't this what you want first thing in the morning?

Lia nodded enthusiastically.

They opened a little after eight. Lia was relieved to see the man with the laptop bag was gone. Then, the steady stream of commuters. The first customers were always in a rush, placing their orders in clipped tones, eyes locked on their phone screens. At her interview, Lia had said she was a people person, because it sounded like the right thing to say. Fiona had nodded and made a mark in her notebook that looked like a big tick. But the job had in fact concretized Lia's knowledge that she was the opposite of a people person. Even though the interactions were mostly brief and uninteresting, she still felt like she'd been physically assaulted after a shift on the till. She much preferred making coffee. She liked the repetitive nature of the work. Once she got into a rhythm she could lose herself in it. Her mind would glaze over as she tamped down the coffee grounds and watched the brown liquid trickle out of the portafilter. It was like meditating, except she got paid to do it.

Another order was placed. Cora stuck another orange Post-it note on the coffee machine: *Decaf almond cortado*.

Famous person alert.

Lia turned around. The girl Cora was serving was about their age, early twenties or so. Lia didn't recognize her, but she didn't doubt that the girl was famous. Her body was clad in skintight Lycra: clean lines, no wobbles or bulges. Her trainers were grape purple, a big, leopard print tick on the side: a defiant YES. The air in the coffee shop had changed. Everyone was looking, but trying not to be seen to be looking, at the girl. Lia turned back to the coffee machine and began to make the girl's drink. She understood why people liked to look at the girl's face. It was pleasant enough, but it was also very generic, a Barbie-type face in that it was not exactly beautiful but was without any obvious faults.

Decaf almond milk cortado? Lia said.

Thank you *so* much! The girl beamed at her. She spoke with a hard enthusiasm that felt rehearsed and oddly empty, as though she didn't mean what she said at all. Cora and Lia watched as the girl was stopped not once but twice on her way out of the cafe. First by a young woman in gym clothes, then by a frazzled mum with a small fat baby tied to her chest, each of them flushed with a mixture of embarrassment and joy.

What's she famous for? Lia asked.

Instagrammer, Cora said, peeling the plastic lid from one of the granola pots. Don't you follow her?

No. I barely use my Instagram.

Cora licked the lid and watched Lia with narrowed eyes. Really? Or are you just saying that?

I've never got into it.

Huh. Well, I've been using it a lot recently. To promote my work. I've got quite a few followers now. It's how I got the bikini job.

Cora had studied at the same art school as Lia, but she graduated last year. Alongside working at the cafe, she did a bit of photography. Mostly headshots for actors she knew. She said the money wasn't bad, even though she had to do a lot of them for mate's rates. Sometimes Lia watched as Cora scrolled through the photographs on her break, selecting the ones she would edit and binning the others. All those hopeful, bright faces, trying out different expressions, different postures, as though the right pose might land them a life-changing role. Most recently, Cora had been on a trip to Barcelona to take photographs for a bikini company. Lia looked them up on the internet. The bikinis were ugly, over the top and garish – that seemed to be their main selling point. The photos were technically good, but Lia didn't understand why the models were looking at their phones in every photo. It must have been some sort of statement or quirky-cool artistic choice that she simply didn't get.

Maybe I should try harder with it.

Maybe you should. And you should follow Sara. Her page is all about positivity and gratitude and making the most of your time or whatever. It sounds cheesy but it's not. It's like, really inspirational.

Through the glass front of the cafe they could see a group of girls sat at the tables outside, phones in hands, hunched over themselves as though they'd like to fold up flat and slip away entirely. When Sara walked past, their heads turned in her direction, flowers towards a sun.

The morning rush was over. There would be a lull until lunch. Cora took out her laptop and set it on the edge of the counter. She was scrolling through Twitter on one tab and looking at sunglasses on the other. Lia took her phone out of her pocket and ran a Google search. Sara's face appeared immediately, her eyes big and blue, blonde hair blowing out around her face.

Sara. Positive energy can change your life ☼ *I'll show you how* 😊 👏 *3x Bestselling Author of the Positive Vibes books, link below!* 📖 ✨

Lia selected a post at random, and a caption appeared:

I'll never get tired of saying this to you guys, but breakfast is the most important meal of the day! Don't forget to fuel your body for a productive day ahead! 🍓 🥞 ✨ *Now that's what I call a breakfast for champions! Remember to show the world your biggest smile today. Like I always say, positive vibes bring positive results* 😊 🍓

There was something childlike and faintly embarrassing

about Sara's unrestrained enthusiasm. But she must have been doing something right. She had more than 600,000 followers on Instagram – a number that seemed enormous, outsized, one Lia could barely comprehend. She googled the capacity of Wembley Stadium: 90,000. Sara had more followers than six full Wembley Stadiums. It was hard not to think about how much that was worth in monetary terms.

Lia clicked through to her own neglected Instagram page. She had posted only five images, including one of her mother's dog and another of a fork resting on a plate, which she had dimmed and brightened and saturated within an inch of recognizability. She deleted it. Sara's page was a neat grid of images, bright and balanced like a lovingly tended flower border. There were numerous plates of food, all healthful and primarily green. Sara in impossible yoga poses. Sara in a bikini. Sara on a yacht. Sara in a mirror. Sara at the gym. A particular shade of bright chlorine blue recurred through the images, tying the profile's aesthetic together. It was impressive, from a compositional perspective. As she scrolled through the posts, Lia noticed the main colour fade from blue to pale yellow. Everything was planned, orchestrated down to the finest detail, and yet each post felt so spontaneous. *Just got in from the gym... Just wanted to let you guys know... How are we all feeling today?* It was like having a friend in your pocket.

Cora peered over Lia's shoulder.

It's good, right?

Yeah. I like it. Great colours.

I can lend you her book, if you want. I've got the first one.

All right.

I think it'll be useful for you. It might give you some tips for handling criticism.

Lia stiffened.

I don't mean that specifically you need it, Cora added hastily. Not necessarily. But everyone needs to be able to like, maintain a sense of self-worth when they're having their art criticized all the time, right?

.   .   .

The week before, Lia's tutor had performed an impromptu critique of everyone's works in progress. She had known her work wasn't ready yet – it was 'in progress', after all – but she had been hoping for some encouraging feedback. She hadn't expected him to hate it.

It doesn't *mean* anything, Matteo said.

Lia picked at the skin around her nails. She could feel eyes on her from all around the room, peeking out from behind canvases and sketchbooks, glancing around work-station corners.

I mean, it's pleasant enough. I can't fault your technique. But I don't know *why* you've done this. What are you trying to make the viewer *feel*?

Matteo tried to make eye contact with her, but Lia's gaze remained fixed on her own inadequate work of art.

This is just a quirky painting of the Millennium Bridge. Something I might buy in a gift shop, or along the South Bank. I have to ask, is that what we're trying to do here?

Matteo turned to face the room. Are we here to make trinkets for gift shops?

A soft titter spread around the room. Lia burned.

You can do better.

His words stung. Lia had researched and mixed that palette of colours for weeks. She spent hours and hours, full days even, down by the bridge. She took photos and sketches, viewed it from every possible angle, in different weather, different light... She put in the work. She fully immersed herself in her subject. Isn't that what Matteo had told them to do?

At the station next to her, Gabby chewed her lip. She was wearing a cardigan several sizes too big, bobbly leggings and a pair of green Crocs. Gabby's project was, as far as Lia could tell, just a pile of dismembered dolls. Matteo got down on the ground to take a closer look, his brow furrowed in concentration.

This is striking stuff, Gabby. I appreciate the layers. From a distance, we are horrified. We almost want to look away altogether. Then when we get closer... well. There's something poignant about this piece close-up. It invites the viewer in... Yes, there's something special going on here. I look forward to seeing where this goes.

When Matteo moved on, Gabby glowed pink and put her hand over her mouth to conceal her enormous smile. Others around the room tried to catch her eye; someone gave her a thumbs up. They wanted to put themselves in proximity to that kind of feedback, that kind of genius.

What to do after feedback like that? Lia had waited a few minutes, then packed up, turned her paintings face

down and left. She stopped on the pavement outside the
art building. People rushed past with speed and purpose, but
she had nowhere to go. She thought about going back to
her shared house. Her bedroom was so small that her desk
was practically wedged up against the bed. But at least the
room was clean. In the bathroom, the walls were peeling,
and the shower drain was clogged with nests of other people's hair. The last time she had yanked one out, it had been
the size and shape of a rat.

She'd checked her phone. It was nearly six o'clock.
At home, her mother would be in the kitchen, chopping
something at the marble-topped island. She might look out
at the sky dimming above the lawn and wonder whether
she should bring the laundry in before making dinner. Her
brothers would be at their clubs – swimming or comput-
ing – or they'd be lounging on the overstuffed linen sofas,
eating crisps and playing on their Nintendo Switch. The
cleaner would have been by now: the carpets would have
perfectly straight vacuum lines across them, like the stripes
on a football pitch.

Lia had walked through the park. The air had a damp,
mineral smell. The sky above her turned lilac and the tem-
perature dropped a few degrees. She thought about the
Millennium Bridge. It would look stunning in this light,
the river flecked with violet and gold, St Paul's lit up like a
Christmas tree, the slow creep of night. But so what? What
was it for? What did it mean? Nothing. Nothing at all. In
the end, she went back to the cafe, where Cora was still
cleaning up. Cora was an artist; Cora would understand.

Look, she'd said. You've absolutely got this. You're super-talented. You can do anything you put your mind to. You know that, right?

Lia had nodded.

But at the same time… If you want to survive art school, you'll have to toughen the fuck up. Just get back on the horse, try again. You can do it, Lia. I believe in you.

.   .   .

The monthly magazine order arrived. Lia tore open the latest copies of *Vogue*, *Good Housekeeping*, *Cosmopolitan* and *National Geographic* and fanned them out on the low table by the window. She collected the old magazines and was about to throw them in the bin, but she stopped. She flicked through them instead; she gazed at all the faces, the sleek bodies.

A notification popped up on Lia's phone screen: *@saraspositivevibes started a live video. Watch it before it ends!* The video stuttered to life. Sara was speaking to the camera and walking down the street at the same time, an act that seemed strangely impressive. Didn't she worry about people looking at her? Didn't she worry about tripping up or knocking into someone? There were people streaming past in the background, but Sara appeared to navigate them with ease. It was clear she did this on a regular basis. She was calm, relaxed, effortlessly flawless. The audio connected mid-sentence:

…because the thing is, we learn most from those who bring us up, not those who bring us down. It is so incredibly important

to surround ourselves with positive people and avoid those neg-
ative people who like to chip, chip, chip away at us until we feel
completely worthless. Yes! I see you all commenting, saying you
know those people... Your sister. Your boyfriend. Your boss. We
all know those people. But listen to me. Life is too short to be
surrounded by people who don't make you feel good. Spending
time with them is not serving you in any way! They do not fill
your life with positive vibes. And on this account, as my long-
time followers will know, we live for positive vibes! Anyway,
that's enough from me and my short morning TED talk. I've
just been to the gym for a really yummy yoga class, and now I'm
off for an exciting meeting – but more on that later! Hope you
guys all have a wonderful, positive day. Mwah!

The video cut out, and Lia was returned to Sara's
Instagram profile. She thought about her parents. They'd
wanted her to study medicine or law, and when she'd tried
to explain how important art was to her, they wouldn't
listen. They would love to hear about Matteo's feedback.
They'd love to know she was failing. When she'd told them
she was going to study art against their wishes, her decision
was met with resignation.

Well, her father had said evenly. The only thing to bear
in mind is that we won't be able to pay your allowance if
you accept the offer to study art. Her mother nodded along,
enthusiastic in her agreement.

It would have been gratifying if they had at least *tried*
to forbid her from following her dream. Lia had braced for
drama – shouting or tears, some emotion at least – but there
was none of that. They dropped her off at the station the

day before the semester started. The five of them in the big
car: her mother, father, brothers and the dog. Lia waved at
them before she walked through the gate and they waved
back in unison, all smiles, like something out of a movie.
After she dragged her suitcase onto the platform, she turned
back. But they had already left.

She hadn't been home since Christmas. Her mum had
texted a few times to ask when they could expect her to visit.
The thought of home always filled her with a hopeful warmth
when she thought about the heated floors, the familiar faces
of her family, the absence of nasty smells in the kitchen, but
at the same time she knew it wouldn't be long before the
comments began. Her dad would ask how living in a shared
house was going, and her mother would, at some point, ask
about Lia's diet. It would be under the pretext of care – *I just
want to make sure you're eating properly* – but the subtext
would be that Lia had put on weight or that she looked
unwell. One way or another, it would be deemed that Lia
had failed at the basic task of taking care of herself. Eating
too much or not enough, she would be to blame.

Later that evening, Lia sat on her bed and opened the magazines. With her scissors, she scraped around each model
and actress, all the beautiful famous people, and laid them
on her blue gingham sheets. There was Gigi Hadid strut-
ting down the catwalk in a sheer black dress, pink flowers
bunched around her waist; Adwoa Aboah in a red leather
trench coat; Rihanna wearing a sequinned, floor-length
gown; Cara Delevingne lying naked in some sort of puddle,

a bottle of perfume clasped in her hand. Lia reached out to touch them. They crinkled under her fingertips. She sliced them into parts – Gigi's long legs now free of her body; Adwoa's head floating beside it – and she cut and cut and cut until her bed was covered with scraps of paper and body parts. What was she doing? She didn't know exactly. She moved the parts around, rearranging them over and over like she was playing a game of Tetris. She was only messing around, taking the women apart and putting them back together, seeing what happened. She felt like it meant something, or could mean something. But how would she articulate what she'd done to Matteo?

But what does it mean? Lia imagined him asking her in front of the group. *What are you trying to say?*

When she showed a photo of the collage to Cora on their next shift together, Lia watched her face carefully, hoping for that flicker of jealousy, that recognition of genius she'd seen on her classmates' faces when they saw Gabby's work. But there was nothing.

Cora raised an eyebrow and shrugged.

It's not bad, she said, zooming in on Lia's phone screen with two fingers. I think I get the concept. It's supposed to be like, feminism, right? Reclaiming their bodies from the pages of the magazine?

Lia thought that sounded right. She nodded.

It's not the worst but it's not the best. Do you know what I'm saying?

Lia nodded.

I think you can come up with something better.

The next day, Lia arrived at the cafe to find that Cora wasn't there. Alejandro was behind the counter, starting up the coffee machine. It spat and hissed.

Lia! Long time no see.

Hey.

Lia looked around. Alejandro had done most of the set-up jobs already, the milk jugs strewn haphazardly across the tabletops. She looked closer. He hadn't swapped out the dying flowers. He had stuffed the fresh flowers in there too, among the ones that were dried out or wilting, had lost half of their petals. It bothered her, like an itch she couldn't reach, but she would have to endure it. Instead, she picked up the box of croissants and began arranging them in the display cabinet, putting the best ones up front.

Throughout the day, she read through more of Sara's posts. They always contained some sort of positive affirmation, something like: *Every new day is a new opportunity to be positive* 😎 ☼ ✧. She looked at Cora's page too, which, she was surprised to see, contained photos of plates of food like kale and lentils, and perhaps even more surprisingly, photos of Cora's own face alongside her photography and digital art. Lia had never seen her like that, carefully made up, smiling broadly. The most recent post was an artwork. It was a photo of her street sign, copied out nine times in different pastel shades. Lia read the caption: *Feeling creative today #grateful #arteveryday #positivevibes*. Cora had almost a thousand followers.

Lia ventured out to attend a talk at the university. It was a guest lecture, given by a famous woman photographer who had recently won a prestigious prize. The auditorium was full. Lia took one of the last seats, sandwiched against a stranger on the end of a row. The lights dimmed; hush fell. The woman lit up. She wore all black and a pair of glasses with thick black rims. Her hair was slicked back but sprung free at the nape of her neck. She tapped her laptop and the projector blinked to life. Words appeared on the screen:

IS IT REAL?

The woman didn't say hello or introduce herself the way lecturers usually did. She tapped her laptop once more and a series of photos appeared, one after the other. Donald Trump standing alongside the Ku Klux Klan, Kim Kardashian in the process of giving birth, Queen Elizabeth sitting on the toilet. Titters from the audience. The laughter petered out and the woman moved centre stage.

Some of these things happened, some of them didn't. But does it matter that the photos are manipulated? Does it change how we perceive them?

The audience was rapt, hanging on her every word.

How often do we question the images around us? How do we define reality?

Lia peered at the faces around her, expecting to find her own bafflement reflected in someone else's expression, but no. She seemed to be the only one that didn't get it. This was the kind of thing she would expect to see on some dodgy blog or Reddit thread, or perhaps on Instagram, but not in an art school.

The culture we live in is saturated with images. In the news, on the Tube, on social media. It is up to us to pay closer attention to what is in front of us.

·　　·　　·

Cora wasn't at work the next day, or the day after that. Lia sent messages, but they went unanswered.

Weren't u supposed to be in today?

Missing u at work lol.

Hey, you were supposed to lend me that positive book.

Oi, where are you?

Lia tried asking Alejandro, who had taken over most of Cora's shifts, but he didn't know – or care.

I dunno babe, she's probably just busy.

In her most recent post, Sara reclined across a pink velvet armchair, a glass of champagne in her hand: *Cheers to the weekend* 😊 🍾. The comments underneath read the same as usual: *You are such a beautiful person, inside and out; U R such an inspiration, thank U; I tried to buy the top you are wearing from Zara, but it's already sold out* 😔.

Eventually, Cora messaged back: *Sorry. Been busy. See u soon. I'll bring the book. X*

Lia's mum texted her a photo of the dog: *Coco can't wait to see you this weekend! She's missing you.* Lia deleted the message. She hated the dog. The dog did not miss her. It was so small and yappy and unnecessary. Lia imagined it sitting on the armchair where she used to sit every evening after school, watching trash on telly and eating snacks delivered by her mother. She imagined its head resting on its fluffy brown and white paws, its eyes closed, perfectly content.

. . .

Three days later, Lia was polishing the cutlery from the glasswasher while she was waiting for the coffee machine to warm up.

Cora came through the back door, late as usual. Hey, she said breezily, as though she'd just returned from popping to the shops. Cora's face was bare of make-up. It looked fresh and dewy, like she'd been doing a lot of sleeping. Her hair was pushed back from her face with a floral print headband.

The shift went slowly. It was raining. Lia wiped down the table and looked out at the park, all smudged and wet through the window like an impressionist painting. When she tried to talk to Cora, she felt her close off, like she was receding back inside her shell. If she asked her a direct question, Cora's answer was vague and she looked at Lia with a faraway, slightly mystified expression, as though she had forgotten who Lia was and didn't understand why she was talking to her at all.

Throughout the afternoon, the rain steadily intensified. By the time she got back to her house that evening, Lia was soaked. There was a rumble of thunder. Lightning cracked across the sky. She sat at her desk, squashed in against her bed, and looked through her folder. The cut-up women were still in there, loose among the pages. She had never stuck them down, nor thrown them away. The photos she had shown Cora were just temporary arrangements. She thought about what Cora had said: *You can come up with something better.* But what if she couldn't? What if this was it, the extent of her creativity? Would that be so bad?

She thought of Matteo's enthusiasm for Gabby's work. Wasn't this a bit like that? A bit surprising, a bit different, but with an important meaning. Or at least there was a meaning that could be applied to it.

Lia opened Instagram. People celebrating, on holiday, making big announcements. Sara had posted a new image of herself doing yoga on a beach, in the peachy glow of a sunrise. Her leggings and sports bra were the exact same colour as the sea. The caption said:

Start now. Start today. Start here. Start with all your doubts and fears inside you. Start and don't give up. Start now and don't stop. Start today guys – I believe in you! A more positive you is just around the corner. Namaste 🙏 🏄 ✨

Lia looked at Sara's face, trying to figure out how she might transform herself in the same way. It wasn't the clothes, the money, the megawatt smile. It was the self-assurance, the self-love that Lia had no idea how to tap into. Watching Sara made her feel like anything was possible, like she could come away from her Instagram page and truly invest in herself. But when Sara was gone and she was facing herself in the mirror, the task in front of her seemed impossible and overwhelming. Lia was trying; she would try harder.

She was about to exit the app when something caught her eye – something she almost recognized, in an off-kilter way, like a doppelganger or a ghost. She enlarged the image, which had been posted from Cora's account. Lia gasped. Her screen flooded with monstrous women, reduced to their parts, and built back up again. They were horrifying and unnatural. They made her recoil, but they also made her want to keep looking. Cora had more than three thousand followers now. Lia clicked on one of the images and read the caption: *Let's reclaim these women from the pages of magazines #fuckthemalegaze #feministvibes #womensmarch.*

Lia looked steadily at her phone screen for a full minute then switched it off. She threw her folder across the room. It clattered against the wardrobe, sending slips of paper drifting through the air like snowflakes. One of her housemates yelled through the wall:

Can you not? I'm trying to sleep!

. . .

Lia was supposed to be meeting with Matteo the next day to talk about her project for the work in progress exhibition, but she knew she wouldn't be able to go through with it. Outside, the streets were glossy and the air still damp, water pooling along the path. But there was a warmth in the air, as though the sun was trying to shine through thick cloud.

The cafe had not long opened when Lia walked in. There was a queue of people stretching out the door.

Oh, hey Lia, said Alejandro. What are you doing here?

I need to talk to Cora.

Little busy here, Lia, Cora said. Can you come back later? She handed a customer their coffee.

I need to talk to you now.

Cora looked up with narrowed eyes. Lia! Come on. I'm working?

A woman with a white bob was watching their conversation and shaking her head.

It's important.

Alejandro looked around. Everything okay, Lia?

I need to talk to Cora.

Cora shrugged. Fine. I'll just tell these customers to wait, shall I?

Excuse me? said the woman with the bob. Excuse me!

Alejandro stepped forward, a smile ready. Hi there! Can I help?

Cora stalked across the cafe and waited for Lia by the window. Well? she said. What is it? What do you want?

Lia opened her mouth to speak, and felt her anger slowly fizzle out. What did she want exactly? Did she want Cora to take the pictures down? Did she want an apology? She didn't know.

Lia? Look, whatever's going on, you need to make it quick. Alejandro can't do it all by himself.

You... You stole my idea, Cora. I trusted you.

I did what?

The magazine cut-ups, Lia said. I showed you the photo. The other day, remember? I was asking for your thoughts. I didn't think you would –

Wait, Cora interrupted. You think my new work is based on your idea?

Well, yeah. I mean, I don't think so... I know –

Do you have any idea how ridiculous this is? My work is *nothing* like yours. I'm sorry you're going through some sort of artistic crisis. I feel for you, I do. But this is incredibly inappropriate... I mean, this is my – our – place of work.

I'm not going through an artistic crisis! It was my idea, and you took it.

Oh, grow up, Cora snapped. This isn't a playground. This is the real world. Now fuck off. Seriously. This is unbelievably out of order.

Cora –

I mean it, Lia. Don't make me phone Fiona.

Lia faltered. Then Cora was back behind the counter, murmuring in Alejandro's ear. His eyes widened in shock. Lia turned and left the cafe as fast as she could. What would she do now? What would Sara do?

Lia opened Instagram. Cora's collages were being shared among women attending a protest that weekend. There were more hashtags emerging: #reclaimthebody #fuckmagazines #burnitdown. Cora had four thousand followers now, a number that was steadily increasing. Meanwhile, Lia's page sat bare, untouched and unnoticed. She sat on a bench in the middle of the park. It was still wet; the chill seeped through her jeans. She clicked onto the post with most likes and typed out a comment:

THIEF!!! SHE STOLE THIS IDEA FROM ME. THIS IS NOT AN ORIGINAL IDEA.

She refreshed the page and saw a response: Bitter much? Get a life. Then another: This isn't about you. This is bigger *than you.* And another: *So what?* Lia scrambled to delete her comment, to wipe it from Cora's page before anyone else saw it, but without warning, Cora's posts vanished. So too did her profile image, post count and follower count. The grid area where her photos used to appear was empty except for the words *No Posts Yet.* For a brief, dizzying instant, Lia thought maybe she had done this, that Cora had been suspended for plagiarism, but no. It dawned on her that she had been blocked.

What else could she do? Her blood was burning with possibilities. She could report Cora – properly, officially – to Instagram for the things she had done. She could report her for things she hadn't done, too. What could get a person banned from Instagram? She could Photoshop Cora's face onto a porn star's body. She could manipulate a photo of Cora naked, defiled, committing a crime. She could leak it onto the internet, in some dark, dank corner, and wait for Cora's life to fall apart. No one would hire her to be their photographer, not even the actors whose headshots she was taking for next to nothing. Maybe she should make it her art school project: the 'Fuck you, Cora' project. What would Matteo think of that? Would it mean anything? Would it have layers? Would it invite the viewer in?

Lia stopped. She caught sight of herself in the window of an abandoned clothes shop. The glass was covered in a crinkly metallic material; a poster advertising a closing-down sale was still dangling in the corner. Her face was distorted like she was trapped in a funhouse mirror, but the reflection was still clearly her, Lia, her face twisted with anger. What would Sara say if she could see her now, like this? Lia thought back to something Sara had said in a recent post. The act of smiling releases certain hormones in your body. You can literally force yourself to be positive if your mind won't cooperate. *Even when you're feeling sad or angry or hurt, you can connect to your inner positive vibes. Just give it a try! Your body will thank you.*

She stopped and took a breath. Her anger faded a little. It had begun to feel distant, as though it belonged to someone else. She tried a smile. Just a small one at first. *The brain doesn't know whether you're faking it, or genuinely over the moon about something, so why not tell it you're feeling good and see what happens?* Lia felt her heart rate slow. It felt miraculous that she had this much control over her own body, her own feelings. *Smiling can even make you live longer.* Sara giggled and tossed her curls. *It's unbelievable, isn't it? We have the power to make ourselves happier and healthier – we have the power to actually extend our lives – and so many people don't make the effort to be positive. Stick with me, guys, and I'll show you how. Mwah!*

Lia breathed in and out. She smiled at herself, wider and wider, until she was beaming, showing all her teeth. The rage was still there, but it had taken on a new shape. It could be boxed up, pushed down. Her body flooded with something else. What was it? Calm? Exhaustion? Emptiness? Maybe the feeling was happiness. Her cheeks began to ache. Her lips cracked, but she didn't stop. On the street behind her, people went by, on their way to their jobs, their friends, their families, their busy lives. She stayed there for a few more minutes, looking herself in the eye, until she was sure she felt completely happy. Then she took one last deep breath and began to walk home.

On the way, Lia passed the university building. Weak sunlight flashed against its cold, shiny surfaces. It occurred to her that Matteo was in there, right now, waiting for her to show up for their meeting. She could go in there and tell him she was struggling. She could ask for help. But she wouldn't do that. Instead, she would go back to her house and look at herself in the mirror. She would stretch and perhaps meditate. She would think positive thoughts. She would put on a little bit of make-up and a nice top. She would take a great photo of herself smiling, sunshine glowing through her bedroom window, and she would post it on Instagram. Then she would wait for the likes to flood in.

Triangulation

Tell me something about you that nobody else knows.

Georgia rolled over to look at Jas: her long body wrapped in a white sheet, early evening sun slicing through the window, brilliant and hot. It looked as though she could catch fire.

Make it good, Jas added. Something special, something secret. Something only you and I will know.

Jas's face was flushed. She looked open and vulnerable, like a small, soft animal. Georgia turned her gaze upwards to the crusted Artex swirls on the bedroom ceiling. She knew what Jas was after. Something thrilling and difficult, a childhood trauma or a deeply held regret. Something cruel she had done, or something unforgivably stupid. But there was nothing like that, so she told her silly things instead. Like: the part of her own body she hated most was the fleshy mole on the inside of her left thigh. That she'd eaten three bars of chocolate for lunch. That sometimes she genuinely wondered if it was possible, or even likely, that everything in the world was a product of her own mind, like some kind of extended dream – or nightmare, depending on how you looked at it.

Jas laughed. Trust you to think you're the first one to come up with that. It's called solipsism, you know.

Georgia knew. She had a degree in philosophy. It was something Jas teased her about relentlessly, calling her 'The Philosopher' whenever she thought Georgia was being too clever. In return, she called Jas 'The Zombie', until it began to strike a nerve.

What else? I want more.

Hmm.

These games made Georgia feel uncomfortable. She didn't understand the impulse to gorge on information about other people, as though the accumulation of facts could cement their bond and stave off disaster. The ceiling was speckled with stars Blu-Tacked to the ceiling by a previous tenant, the kind that would once have glowed in the dark.

I prefer the moon to the sun?

But you'd die without the sun.

Not if we're all living in my imagination.

Jas laughed and stroked Georgia's shoulder with the tip of her finger. Georgia was thinking about school, and how she used to get called Moon-Face, like the character from the Enid Blyton *Faraway Tree* stories. Ever since, she'd been sensitive about her round, childish shape. She turned to offer this to Jas, but her face had lost its dreamy, playful expression, hardening into something cold and solid.

Is that what this is all about then? A little project for your narcissism?

Georgia laughed. It echoed slightly; the room laughed back at her.

Jas began to fiddle with the sheet, tugging herself out of its tight embrace. What time does he get back? she asked.

I don't know. Does it matter?

Don't think he'd be too thrilled to find me in his bed, do you?

Georgia stood up. She was naked. It was still warm, but cooling. The sky outside was the palest peach, with a bright slash across the horizon.

Where are you going? Jas asked.

He's out. I don't think he'll be back till late.

Georgia edged around the bed without looking at Jas. She could feel eyes on her, sweeping over the dimples on the backs of her thighs, the halo of frizz on the top of her head. Georgia tried not to speak about Jonathan in front of Jas, which was difficult – they did live together – but Jas always found a way to bring him up. She sneaked him into conversations, whatever they were speaking about. *Did Jonathan buy you those new jeans? Does Jonathan like drinking wine too? What does Jonathan think?* She would slip it in, like it was natural, like he was just some mutual friend of theirs. Everything would seem fine, but then her face would alter, almost imperceptibly, and the whole room would dim.

Georgia moved down the narrow corridor and into the kitchen. The floor was vinyl – fake terracotta tiles, too shiny and too orange – and the cabinets were old; the hinges shrieked whenever opened or closed. The kitchen was at the back of the flat and overlooked the car park. Georgia squinted through the gaps in the blinds: no one out there. She slipped her arms into a jumper that was far too big and started to fill the kettle to make coffee.

Jas appeared in the doorway, arms folded across her bare breasts.

Hello, she said.

Hi. Georgia weighed the grounds of coffee into the cafetière, the way Jonathan had shown her.

Everything all right? Jas wiped her finger along the nearest bookshelf. She collected a scraggy clot of dust and shook it to pieces all over the floor.

Grand, thanks.

Jas nudged Georgia with her hip and took the cafetière out of her hands. That was something they both did – took over ordinary tasks, like cooking or taking out the bins. Especially making coffee; they were both particular about coffee.

Georgia had found Jas with Jonathan. They sat down together on their sofa one evening and scrolled through endless profile pages, black-and-white images of headless naked and nearly naked women in various sexy poses. Georgia wasn't sure why all the photos were black-and-white; perhaps it was to make things look a little classier, or another way to protect the women's identities. Jas's picture was cut off at the chin and below the knees. Her face was a secret, but they could see her beautiful long neck, her sharp collarbone, the gentle curves of her body that, for some reason, made Georgia think of water. They chose her together – their unicorn.

They met her at a pub, a neutral place, a bus ride from their flat. The place was a bit run-down, but in a trendy way: the bar was strung with fairy lights and the shelves stacked with dusty board games and empty gin bottles, a few dried flowers stuck into their necks.

Jonathan chewed on his thumbnail while they waited for Jas to arrive. Should we have asked for a photo of her face too? I mean, she's got our faces. It's only fair.

Georgia thought about the idea of Jas 'having' their faces, as though she was taking something from them, droopy pockets of skin, and they would be left with nothing but soft flesh, wet and red raw.

She's a woman on her own. We have to give her *something* over us.

Yeah, but she's chosen to be here, hasn't she? We're not exactly forcing her.

Jonathan could be unsympathetic when it came to other women. He made a show of listening intently when Georgia railed about rapists and murderers and workplace sexism, but he was suspicious of anything that involved what he perceived to be a choice. He'd become almost apoplectic when Georgia used the phrase 'emotional labour' for the first time, especially when she said she wouldn't be buying the birthday presents for his mum and sister any more.

Georgia and Jonathan?

They turned around. Jas. She was wearing a floaty dress covered with a bright, multicoloured print that looked like confetti, a black leather jacket and a pair of shiny Doc Martens. Her thick, wavy hair was pinned loosely on the top of her head, and she wore heavy flicks of eyeliner, like Amy Winehouse. Georgia was surprised to see her standing there, real and solid. Had she thought, deep down, that Jas wouldn't show up? That she would remain a shared fantasy between her and Jonathan? But she was here now, in real life, a woman who truly did want to have sex with both of them at the same time. Georgia's body flashed with heat, desire and trepidation curdling in the pit of her body. It was not unlike coming down with an illness. Should she stand up and give Jas a hug? Shake her hand? There was a curious intimacy in the fact that they had all traded messages for a few weeks, including photographs of their naked bodies.

Jonathan stood up to give Jas a kiss on the cheek. It wasn't an air kiss or a brush of cheeks. Georgia watched, enthralled, as the soft flesh of his lips lingered against the smooth skin of Jas's face. Her heartbeat flickered. Jonathan leaned his face close to Jas's and asked her what she'd like to drink, then he went to the bar. Jas perched on the edge of the leather banquette where, moments earlier, Jonathan had been sitting and stressing, an entirely different person from this new, cool and flirtatious one. Georgia was taken aback by the abrupt change, but she wasn't angry, mostly intrigued and vaguely turned on. She looked at Jas, who was fussing with her dress and looking out around the bar. Looking everywhere, it seemed, except at her.

So... You found the bar okay?

It was a stupid thing to say. The words hovered accusingly, and Georgia saw Jas's face twitch briefly.

Yeah, I've been here before, so...

Oh, do you live around here?

Jas looked Georgia directly in the eye.

Shit, sorry. I'm not supposed to ask that, am I?

Georgia felt the balance shifting, creaking out of her favour. Jas leaned back and looked steadily at Georgia. The nervous energy she had possessed before fizzled out, like a match held underwater.

No, you're not.

Jas's voice was blunt, almost bored. Georgia searched her face for a smile, a trace of warmth, but Jas held her gaze, steady and impenetrable.

They took their coffees through to the living room and sat on the old, sagging sofa, which was covered in brightly coloured cushions and throws. The first time Jas had been to the flat, she raised her eyebrows at their decor: the rugs with zigzags and diamond shapes, the cream fabric wall hanging, the Argos lamp. Georgia asked what was wrong, and Jas only said that she liked what they'd done with the place. But Georgia could tell there was something unsaid, and indeed, it came out months later, during an argument, when Jas announced that she found their abundant cultural appropriation distasteful. Georgia hadn't understood and felt stupid, later googling 'cultural appropriation' and reading article after article. It had never occurred to her that the patterns they chose to decorate their home with were inspired by Indigenous American art, and even if it had, it would never have occurred to her that it might be wrong. She wanted to talk to Jonathan about it, for reassurance or backup, but she knew he would roll his eyes and she would feel herself dimming.

How's the coffee?

It's good, thanks.

Better than when Jonathan makes it? It is, isn't it?

Yes.

I knew it.

Jas was still naked. She stretched her arms above her head and tensed her body into a hard line, balanced against the sofa. She was showing off. The taut muscles in her thighs were formed not through repetitive gym hours but team sports like netball and football, activities Georgia despised. Georgia wanted to touch her; she wanted to tell her to put some clothes on, but she knew she couldn't. Jas was on the edge of a bad mood, and she didn't want to push her over completely.

Georgia took a sip of her coffee. A small, dark shape darted across the floorboards behind the sofa. She screamed.

Jas leaped up onto the sofa and looked around. What? What is it?

There was something... It's gone behind the sofa. It looked like a rat!

A rat!

Jas sounded thrilled, as though this were great fun, some stupid prank. She peered behind the sofa. She wiggled the floor lamp this way and that until the shape shot across the room and disappeared into the kitchen. Georgia shrieked again and burst into tears.

It's just a mouse, Jas said flatly.

Georgia took out her phone.

What are you doing?

I'm phoning Jonathan.

Don't do that. Come on. It's okay.

Jas wrapped her arms around Georgia and hugged her close, tight against her chest. It was warm; too warm.

Georgia couldn't breathe. She swatted Jas away.

What's your problem? Don't fucking hit me.

I didn't hit you – I couldn't breathe!

I was trying to comfort you.

You were smothering me!

Are you serious?

Look, I'm just upset, I –

No, no. It's fine. I'll go. Call your boyfriend to come and take care of you.

No! Jas... Please.

Things were unravelling so fast. Georgia thought about begging Jas to stay. She could smooth things over, the way she usually did. But she was tired, and she was still thinking about the creature in the house. How had it got in? Would it come back? Were there more of them?

The front door slammed. Jas was gone. Georgia's thumb hovered over Jas's name in her contacts list. She knew she should call her and beg her to come back. That was the quickest way to resolve things between them. But she realized, with startling clarity, that Jas's presence wouldn't make her feel safe. She wanted Jonathan.

Jonathan answered the phone in a sing-song voice.

Heeeeey, Georgieeee! How's it going?

Georgia could hear thumping music, people cheering and laughing. She imagined Jonathan bathed in blue light in the middle of a nightclub, even though, from what he'd told her of his plans earlier, he was more likely in someone's dimly lit living room.

I'm okay! I'm okay! Are you having a nice time?

You don't sound okay.

Don't I? Oh, well. That's strange.

Jonathan hesitated on the other end of the line and the party sounds began to fade. They were replaced by the purring sound of a car creeping past, the low hoot of a nighttime bird. There was a rustling sound as he adjusted the phone against his ear, perhaps the faint whisper of a sigh.

Do you need me to come home?

What? Why would you say that?

I can tell something's wrong.

Georgia said nothing and looked out of their window at the city in darkness, the ghostly outline of her own face reflecting back at her.

It's nothing. I just wanted to hear your voice.

Jonathan inhaled sharply through his nose. I'll see you in half an hour.

When Jonathan arrived, Georgia was sitting on the sofa with her feet up, her arms wrapped around her knees. Her face was red and blotchy, but she was no longer crying. She told him about the creature as he made her a cup of camomile tea. He said it was probably a mouse, but Georgia insisted it couldn't have been; it was far too big. She apologized for interrupting his night. He said it was fine. Eventually, Georgia got under the covers and curled into the solid warmth of Jonathan's body. Every time she closed her eyes, all she could think of was rats, lots of rats, so many of them, moving over each other in such a way that it was impossible to tell where one rat ended and another began. A giant, shifting mass of rats; dark matted fur; long, slinky, wormlike tails, and every so often a glint from one of hundreds of beady black eyes.

·　　·　　·

When Georgia explained her job to other people, they always seemed to imagine she worked in some kind of factory. But the cookies weren't baked in some huge, shiny industrial oven, they were baked in Denise's home kitchen, in a regular oven. She made them two or three at a time, maybe four if they were all smaller-sized cookies, and during busy periods, like Valentine's Day, she could be baking all day long. It was Georgia's job to ice each cookie with the correct personalized message then put it in a presentation box with a clear cellophane window. Denise checked everything before someone else – another girl – packed the cookie into a box and posted it. Georgia had never met her. Their paths never crossed.

Sometimes Denise was around when Georgia was working, bustling between the rooms, ready to make cups of tea and chat through the orders. Other times, the house was empty, and Georgia had to make her own way through the main corridor, past the laundry room, the bathroom, the living room and the high-ceilinged hallway, and into the back room that had once been a grand dining room but was now, since the divorce, the room Denise used for her cookie business.

Against the back wall, a large, walnut table, covered with a plastic polka-dot tablecloth and eight matching chairs. This was where she did the icing. There were two desks on the other side of the room, where Denise did all the business paperwork, mostly on her own but sometimes with her accountant. The remaining space was taken up by large black shelving units, on which there were various dry ingredients and different styles of box. Georgia selected an appropriate box based on the message and the size of the particular cookie. Usually the messages Georgia iced were pretty standard: *Happy birthday, Susan! I'm sorry! Get well soon, Johannes! Congratulations on your engagement, Lola and Lee!* But occasionally she'd get a strange one that she wouldn't know how to interpret. *I HOPE YOU'RE HAPPY*, for example, written in all caps. It was sent anonymously, so in theory the recipient would never know who sent the cookie. *I HOPE YOU'RE HAPPY.* Georgia read the words out loud in different tones – sweet and happy, sad and dejected, angry and embittered. It could be any or all of the above, at once kind and sarcastic. How would the recipient feel when they opened the box and saw the cookie but no further message or sender information? Would they be comforted? Would they panic? Would they just eat the cookie?

After packing up the last of the cookies, Georgia stood to leave, but something made her stop. Did something move on the bottom shelf? She swore she could hear rustling, little feet scrabbling against the floorboards. She got down on her hands and knees and shone her phone torch beneath the table, blood pounding in her ears. There was nothing there. No scuttling sounds, no moving shapes. After a few minutes, she got to her feet and her vision glittered. She closed her eyes and steadied herself against the table. She left as quickly as she could, phoning Jonathan on her way out.

.　　.　　.

Jonathan found an article online about how to make a trap. It involved slathering peanut butter on an empty drink can, which he placed onto a rod over a bin. He fashioned a sort of ramp out of an old cardboard box. The idea was that the mouse would be tempted by the peanut butter, climb up the ramp to reach it, shuffle along the rod and then, when it stepped onto the can, whoosh! It would lose its balance and fall into the empty bin. The article suggested filling the bin with water so the creature – whatever it was – drowned. Jonathan suggested doing this too, but Georgia didn't want the mouse to die. Drowning seemed like a cruel way to go. She just wanted it caught and moved away, out of her life, as painlessly as possible. When she told him about seeing something at Denise's, Jonathan was concerned.

Are you feeling all right, bun?

He used the nickname he'd had for her since they first got together – bunny, because of her apparently cute nose – even though she had asked him to stop.

Not great.

He nodded and took off his glasses, wiping them clean with the hem of his shirt. Do you think – and don't get cross with me here – but do you think this could be an anxiety thing?

Georgia stared at him. It seemed obvious that it was indeed an anxiety thing.

Of course, Jonathan. It's an irrational fear, a phobia, whatever you want to call it. I know lots of people are chill about rodents, but I'm just not, okay?

No, I know. I know that. I suppose what I meant was… There isn't anything else you're feeling anxious about, is there? Something that might be making this… worse than it maybe is?

You think I'm making it up?

I don't think you're making it up at all. It's just… I dunno. Are you maybe making it mean too much?

Georgia turned away. She took a glass from the cabinet and began filling it with water. I don't know what you're trying to say.

Okay, forget it then. Forget I said anything. You clearly don't want to talk about it.

Talk about what?

Jonathan said nothing; his expression suggested he was experiencing a degree of physical pain.

I'm going out tonight, so you can have the flat to your-self, free from your irritating psycho girlfriend –

That's not fair. That's not what I said.

That's what you meant though, isn't it?

Jonathan left the room. Georgia examined the trap Jonathan had made. She touched the can with her index finger and sent it spinning.

．　　　．　　　．

The next day, Georgia was jolted out of sleep by the sound of the doorbell, a harsh, metallic sound that yanked her from the cosy strangeness of her dream, in which a blue ghost rat was talking from the foot of her bed. It was almost half past three in the afternoon.

She had spent the whole night playing catch-up. When she had arrived, Robyn and Amia were already hammered, and no matter how much Georgia drank, she never seemed to reach their level of inebriation. But based on the sweet-sour stink of her body, still clad in last night's clothes, she must have managed it eventually.

Georgia checked her phone. There was a message from Jonathan, saying he wouldn't be back until later, several from Amia (the only words she could see in the previews were *I'm sorry but…* and *It's not my fault that…*) and none at all from Robyn.

The doorbell sounded again, and Georgia pulled a pillow over her head. It was coming back to her now: Amia sway-ing on the spot under the pastel glow of fairy lights, her hair flapping in the wind. *Georgia has a girlfriend now. She has two of them. Two… you know. Lovers.* Robyn hadn't known about Jas. She'd looked appalled, maybe even angry. But what did it have to do with her? The doorbell jangled a third time. Georgia dragged herself out of bed and put her dressing gown on over her clothes.

She opened the door. Jas. Her face clean and bare and startlingly beautiful. She was wearing a pair of jeans and a hooded sweatshirt.

Can I come in?

Jas didn't say anything about the smeared make-up she clearly hadn't taken off from the night before. She didn't say anything about the rumpled sheets, the musty stench of hangover sweat. She didn't say much at all. She led Georgia to bed, as though everything was normal, and began to kiss her. Jas smelled fresh and clean. Her mouth was minty, and her skin smelled like tropical shower gel – coconuts and pineapple and freshness. Georgia thought about putting a stop to things and taking a shower before they continued, but it felt rude, almost offensive to stop the kissing when the kissing was this good. She felt her body respond to Jas automatically as she slowly let go of the fuzz of anxiety about their relationship, her hangover, her friends, Jonathan. But then it was over, and everything came crashing down like a sheet of water.

Did you fuck him last night? Jas demanded.

Wait, what?

Did you fuck Jonathan last night here, in this bed?

No… I didn't. But even if I did –

You should have told me if you did.

But why? Georgia sat up and pulled the duvet over her chest. What are you talking about? Jonathan's my boyfriend. I thought we were all happy with this. After... After we met, I thought we all agreed...

Georgia's vision speckled. She hadn't eaten or drunk anything at all that day, except for a few sips of old, warm water she'd found in a bottle on the floor by the bed. Jas kept talking but the room was whirling; Georgia couldn't look up at her. Then something slunk out from under the bed. She howled and lunged into the centre of the bed.

Jas's face paled. What the fuck?

Did you see it? It's under the bed. It's there now. Oh my god, I can't. I can't deal with this. I can't.

I didn't see anything, said Jas. And anyway, it's just a... Holy shit.

They both watched as a large rodent, larger than a mouse, bigger even than a rat, scuttled out of the bedroom door and into the kitchen.

Get it! Georgia cried.

Jas leaped up and chased the creature into the kitchen. Behind her, Georgia sobbed. They both watched as the creature disappeared through the dark chasm between the washing machine and the wall.

The pest control company said they would be there in two hours. It felt like an eternity. Georgia was too afraid to stay in the flat, so they went outside in their coats, Jas sitting on the low wall, Georgia pacing, both smoking while Jas tried to calm Georgia down.

It wasn't that big... And it was only one.

Yeah, sure, it wasn't that big. I know you saw it! You can't pretend it wasn't fucking huge.

Okay, okay. It was bigger than I was expecting, but still... It could have been bigger.

How big would you like it to be exactly?

Well, I would like it not to be there at all, obviously, because I don't want you to feel upset, but honestly...

Jas stopped speaking. They both turned to watch as a silver car pulled up in front of them. Jonathan hopped out of the back seat.

What's going on? Why aren't you answering your phone?

Oh shit, said Georgia. Sorry. I didn't think. It was that fucking thing again. I... We both saw it. Jas called pest control. They're on their way.

The mouse again, huh?

It's true, Jas said. I saw it. To be fair, it is pretty big.

Hello there, Jas, Jonathan said. Nice to see you.

Georgia stared hard at the ground. She realized, fleetingly, that she wasn't supposed to have Jas round without asking Jonathan first. She wondered whether he would have figured out that they'd had sex, from the tangled sheets, the smells of their bodies. Would he say anything? Did he care?

Hi, Jas said.

Well, thanks for calling them, Jonathan added, after a long pause.

Sure, no problem. I guess I'll go now. I'll see you soon, George? Okay?

You don't have to –

No, it's fine. I've got stuff to do, and you'll be busy with the… With the pest control people.

Jas waved a hand dismissively and turned down the road towards the station without looking back. Jonathan watched her go, a half-smile on his face, his expression soft and open. Georgia began to prepare her excuses. But what was she supposed to do if Jas turned up out of the blue? It was Jas who had broken the rules, not her. Jonathan went inside to look around the flat before pest control arrived. Georgia sat on the low wall and rolled another cigarette. The sun had almost completely drained from the sky, except for the last few flecks of fire on the horizon. It would be dark soon. She couldn't sleep at home tonight, that was for sure. She was bothered, too, by the fact Jas had left so abruptly. Didn't she realize how terrified Georgia was? Couldn't she have taken Georgia with her?

· · ·

From the minute they met, Jonathan had been besotted with Jas. He returned from the bar with his eyes sparkling, his smile dopey and irrepressible. Georgia thrilled to see it. His desire sent a slow, steady spread of heat through-out her body. Jonathan was giddier than Georgia had seen him in years. Watching him flirt with someone so beau-tiful, and be flirted with in return, filled her with some-thing like inner peace. It felt like an endorsement of her own choices. They left the bar and decided to go back to Georgia and Jonathan's flat. They were having fun; none of them were ready for the night to end. Jas had a small bit of MDMA on her, which they put in their last round of drinks. In the taxi on the way home they were all touching each other in the back seat. Gently, tentatively exploring each other. Jonathan had one arm around Jas and was stroking Georgia's face and neck, the other hand resting on Jas's thigh. Jas had an arm around Jonathan, under his jacket, while Georgia was practically sitting in Jas's lap, touching her legs, her belly, her face. She pulled Jas's face towards her to kiss, but Jas whispered: not yet; not here.

By the time they got upstairs, into the unnervingly familiar territory of their flat, Jas's face had become unreadable. Jonathan wanted to kiss Jas, but she stopped him and said she needed a minute. She went into the bathroom and locked the door. Georgia asked Jonathan if he thought Jas was all right. He said he was sure she was fine.

I can't blame her for getting a little bit of cold feet, he said. But she'll come around.

Georgia and Jonathan had discussed the possibility of sex on the first date, and while they were both open to it, they felt it was unlikely. The website they'd used to find Jas cautioned against sex on the first meeting, but usually as a measure to protect the unicorn. It also said there was nothing wrong with going for it if everyone was comfortable. And they were all comfortable, weren't they? Jas had said she wanted to go back to theirs. She had seemed up for it, hadn't she? In fact, hadn't she been the one to suggest it in the first place? Georgia thought back to the taxi, all the touching. They were all into it, no doubt.

After a few more minutes, Jas emerged from the bathroom. Georgia and Jonathan were sitting side by side on the sofa, like strangers waiting for an appointment with the dentist.

Have you got anything to drink? Jas asked.

Jonathan made them all an old fashioned, and Jas slowly came back into herself, rejuvenated by the alcohol. The other Jas, the mopey and distant one, disappeared.

Later, when they had finished having sex, Georgia glanced at Jas across Jonathan's torso. His arm was still around her, but she was facing away from him, towards the window. She was quiet: probably asleep already. Jonathan was dozing; it wouldn't be long until he fell asleep himself. Georgia wriggled out of his grasp and switched off the light.

.   .   .

Jonathan waved at Georgia from the communal entrance.

Are you coming back inside?

Are you joking?

Jonathan sighed and pinched the bridge of his nose. He walked down the path towards the wall where Georgia was waiting.

Come inside, Georgia. Enough.

I can't! I genuinely can't. You didn't see the size of the thing. It's absolutely –

What are you going to do then? You're going to sit out here all night? You don't think there are more, and bigger, creatures that can get you out here? You're not going to be any safer sitting out here on the street.

Georgia was taken aback by Jonathan's tone – sharp and brusque. He had never spoken to her like that before. They both turned to look at the vehicle spluttering into their cul-de-sac. It was a black van, with the words BUZZ OFF sprayed in yellow. There was a picture of a bumblebee inside the 'O' and underneath, in smaller letters, it said: WE'LL MAKE YOUR PESTS BUZZ OFF.

Buzz off. We'll make your pests buzz off? Jonathan said.

They were the only company who could come tonight. I'm sure they'll be fine.

Maybe I'll go and stay with Alison, Georgia said. She hadn't seen her sister in weeks, but she knew she would be home. Alison had two kids and a full-time job; she couldn't have gone far.

Okay. Yeah. You need anything from the house?

It's fine. I can borrow pyjamas. I've got a shift at Denise's tomorrow. I'll be back in the afternoon.

All right then.

Jonathan raised a hand at the two men who got out of the van. Georgia could already see him constructing a new version of himself, laddish and personable. As she turned towards the bus stop, she heard him say, All right mate? And she knew that within minutes, Jonathan would be explaining that his girlfriend was hypersensitive, an exaggerator, and that the 'rat' was probably not a big deal at all.

·　　·　　·

It rained all night. In the morning, the leaves on the plane trees were glossy and bright. On her way to work,

Georgia passed children wearing yellow welly boots and swinging tiny umbrellas above their heads. It didn't feel that long since her niece and nephew were that size. The time had slipped by almost unnoticeably. When Betty was a newborn – a tiny, curled-up, non-verbal shrimpy thing – Georgia was eighteen, on the cusp of adulthood. Now, six years later, Betty could walk and talk and read and recite her times tables, and what had Georgia done? She'd graduated with a degree in philosophy, met Jonathan, moved into their own flat, and now she was juggling working for Denise with sporadic copywriting work. Did any of this mean anything? Were they achievements? She didn't know. Maybe.

Alison had been drinking last night and, as usual, she wanted to psychoanalyse the effect their parents' divorce had had on them. You know, she said, their relationship is the safe foundation on which we constructed our whole selves. She behaved as though their parents separating was something uniquely traumatic, rather than something that happened to children all the time. Personally, Georgia felt that the divorce had been healthy and had given her realistic expectations of adult relationships. She always hoped to talk to Alison about other things – about Alison's job, her own divorce, how she was finding life as a single mother – but no matter how the conversation started, it always circled back to their parents, with Alison insisting that Georgia had certain feelings about it, deep down, that Georgia was certain she didn't have.

·   ·   ·

Georgia arrived at Denise's and unlocked the door. The house was silent. She didn't play music as she usually did. The night with Alison had put her in a grey, melancholy mood. She tried to focus on the cookies in front of her – *Great job, Shareena!* and *Happy graduation, Courtney!* and *Don't cry because it's over, smile because it happened* – but she was too alert to the sounds around her. The soft scrape of cardboard boxes against each other could be the scratching of rat feet and a creaky door hinge could be them trying to communicate with her. The knot in her stomach felt so solid that she grasped her midriff to see if there was some sort of growth inside her, but no. It was all in her head.

Just after she left Denise's that afternoon, Jonathan phoned.

So, they've found one… he said. But the problem is, they think this one they've caught is a baby and they need to get the mother.

Right, she said, glancing towards the bush in front of her, which had made a rustling sound.

So? What do you think? Are you going to come back tonight, or…

She thought about asking Jonathan if he even wanted her to come back, but she realized she was afraid of what he might say.

No, no. It's fine. I'll go back to Alison's.

Do you need to pick up some stuff?

She'll probably have something I can borrow. Did they say when they think they might catch the big one?

It's a waiting game. It'll happen whenever she takes the bait. The guy said he'd come back in the morning though, so I guess it could be soon.

In the background of the call, Georgia could hear movement. Rustling. Perhaps the sound of socked feet padding across the floorboards. She thought about asking Jonathan if anyone was there with him. But it might just be his own feet moving through the flat, his rustling sounds. But then, did she hear someone say his name? *Jonathan.* It sounded like Jas. She held her breath and waited to hear if she would speak again, but she didn't.

All right. I'll call you in the morning.

Jonathan hung up and Georgia looked down at her phone, his smiling image and the words CALL ENDED. It could have been one of the pest control people speaking to him. Or maybe it was the television, or a podcast playing through the speaker. She navigated away from Jonathan's contact information and towards Jas. An image of Jas's naked torso filled the top half of Georgia's phone screen, nipples winking like a pair of eyes. She should probably change that. She probably should have changed it a while ago. She had thought it was fun, funny, even, a little joke, something to make her smile whenever Jas called or messaged, but now it seemed crass and inappropriate.

It began to rain again, a slow, hazy drizzle that bounced off cars and made them look as though they were glowing with light. The thought of going back to Alison's filled Georgia with dread, but she didn't know where else she could go. She could call Jas, but that would mean rehashing the events of the other night. Jas would need reassurance, apologies. Georgia was getting bored of always being the bad one. Weren't they all adults in this relationship? Hadn't they all agreed to this? Georgia had always preferred it when they were able to spend time as a three. It was Jonathan who had cooled on the whole idea. He said that, for him, it was a one-off thing, but he was encouraging of Georgia and Jas's relationship. In the beginning, he seemed to take pleasure in it. Georgia didn't ask any questions. She'd gone with the flow, done what everybody wanted. So why did it always feel like she was being punished for it?

The skies darkened, and Georgia could see rats everywhere: flashes of bodies shimmying along in the gutter or scrabbling up walls, crawling along the pavement towards her with their sharp teeth bared. She could feel them on her body, the way they'd squeeze up the legs of her dungarees and down between her breasts, the way it would feel to have their thick, furry bodies moving against hers, the slither of their tails, the spikes of their claws. The rain got heavier. Georgia saw a pub on the corner and decided to go inside.

What can I get for you, hun?

The girl behind the bar had a short, pinkish-blonde bob. She was wearing a black T-shirt and a black lacy choker around her neck. On her wrists, she had several braided bracelets – friendship bracelets, they called them when Georgia was at school. She wondered briefly whether the girl had been given them by her friends.

Wine, Georgia said. Large, please.

Any particular kind of wine, or…

Whatever. Red, I guess.

Well, in that case… I recommend the house red. It's a Sangiovese.

Sounds great.

Georgia looked around. The pub was smarter on the inside than it appeared from the outside. She noticed there was a cocktail menu, and the floors appeared to have been freshly waxed. There was hardly anyone in there; somewhat unsurprising, since it was only about four on a Thursday afternoon. The bartender placed the glass of wine on a napkin in front of Georgia.

Rough day?

Kind of.

Georgia was horrified to find her eyes filling with tears. What was she crying about? None of it was that bad. There was nothing she couldn't deal with. She blinked hard and dabbed at the corner of her eye with her jumper sleeve.

I guess I'm hormonal or something.

Aren't we all?

Nancy was easy to talk to. There were various trashy magazines behind the bar, left by another bartender. Nancy read the celebrity gossip aloud to Georgia and they discussed who they liked and who they didn't. Once they had worked through celebrities, they moved on to the shocking real-life stories. There was a story about a couple who had a demon in their house that turned out to be his dead ex-lover. There was a story about a woman who survived a plane crash and had to eat her own sister.

That's fucked, Nancy said. I could never do that.

Do you have a sister? Georgia asked.

No.

Well, you're a better person than me then. I'd eat mine if I had to.

Nancy laughed and Georgia glowed. The bar was dead. Nancy joined Georgia in drinking wine, although she drank hers from a paper coffee cup. Before long, Nancy's shift was over, and Georgia's bill was wiped from the till.

On the house, Nancy said with a wink.

Georgia checked her phone. No messages, not from anyone. The walls around her faltered and she realized she was pretty drunk. Had she suspected all along that Jas and Jonathan were together? Maybe that's where the desire to sleep with Nancy had come from, as some kind of equalizer. But why shouldn't she? Nancy liked her, didn't she? Nancy wanted to. The afternoon's drinking had made the world seems softer and fuzzier, more forgiving. Georgia invited herself back to Nancy's for the night, and Nancy said yes.

.　　.　　.

Georgia woke early the next morning. Nancy's bedroom was bathed in a cold blue morning light. The curtains hadn't been closed before they went to sleep. In fact, there were no curtains at all, just a large, bare window that looked out onto a well-tended garden, a smart set of wooden garden furniture stacked against a wall, ready to be put away for the winter. Georgia had huge blanks in her memory. She remembered talking about eating Alison and she felt like she was going to throw up. It had seemed funny at the time. Nancy had laughed, hadn't she? She couldn't remember anything Nancy had told her about herself. Did she say she was a student? But where? And of what? Georgia tried to pull up more memories of the night before, but everything was scrambled. She had a fleeting memory of being told to wait outside the front door while Nancy went inside to check the coast was clear. She could remember the thick ivy that grew up the side of the house, covering a full side of the building. She could remember the red front door, with one of those posh brass knockers, then she was ushered into a hallway, past a carpeted staircase and into a ground-floor bedroom with posters on the walls. She remembered the two of them giggling and Nancy raising a finger to her lips: shh. Did Nancy still live with her parents?

Lifting the covers, Georgia slowly moved her body out of the bed. She still had her underwear on, which she presumed meant they hadn't fucked. That was something. Her dungarees were tangled up with a pair of Nancy's tights by the foot of the bed. Georgia pulled her phone out of the pocket. She pressed on the screen and tried the power button, but the phone didn't respond. Her throat was dry and scratchy. She had a simmering, dizzy feeling in her stomach, something like dread – but of what? She hadn't done anything wrong. Even if she had slept with Nancy, everyone knew the score: the relationships were open; she wasn't tied down. That was a good thing, wasn't it?

Georgia pulled her jumper over her head, and a gentle clanging sound made her freeze. In the corner of the room, beside a haphazard stack of textbooks, there was a large metal cage filled with brightly coloured toys and ramps and tubes, and there, at the bottom, among the sawdust, gnawing the trapdoor with its large, pointed teeth, was a black-and-white rat. Georgia watched as it turned and scampered into its dark enclosure, its tail flashing pink and fleshy. How had she not noticed last night? She seized her bag and fled from the room and down the hallway, past an open door through which she could hear the low murmur of voices. Georgia grabbed at the lock on the front door – she had to get out, she had to get out immediately – but it was stuck. When she finally got it open, she raced down the path and kept running. She didn't stop until she felt like her lungs would give out.

Intimacy

It was a gaudy poster, unusual for the theatre – two profiles in silhouette, a man and a woman, against a yellow and plum background, the word INTIMACY in thick teal letters – but then again, the play itself was a departure from their usual repertoire. It had been described as a 'searing' and 'darkly funny' drama about two lovers, and had created a stir in Germany before being translated into English for a limited run off-Broadway, which then transferred to Broadway for a longer run. Now here it was, in London. Despite its reputation, there was a lot of scepticism about the play, particularly among the front-of-house staff at the theatre.

Intimacy? Bembe said, with an eyebrow raised. Please. What kind of title is that?

He was lounging in an armchair in the Dress Circle bar, eating a packet of crisps. Danny sat opposite him, rolling a cigarette. Zara was behind the bar. She bent down to take a sip of the flat white she had made for herself on the coffee machine in the main bar downstairs, while Curtis, the bar manager, was sorting out a cash discrepancy at the upper circle bar. They were supposed to pay for anything fancier than a filter coffee. Staff price was only a pound. But still.

Is it about sex? asked Alessandra. It sounds like it's about sex. She was cross-legged on the floor, doing side stretches.

Have you seen the poster? said Danny. It's definitely about sex.

How did you get sex from two darkened faces and some childish colours? said Bembe.

There's no script, said Zara. No one really knows what it's about. But they've used the same poster for all of the productions. Annie's read more about it than me. Haven't you, Annie?

Annie was sat on the floor by the bar, reading. She looked up. I've read a few articles, yeah, she said. But there's not much information out there. It's all pretty cryptic. They've never allowed reviewers in. A few people have written blogs, but they've all been taken down. Something to do with artistic integrity?

Artistic integrity? Bembe said. What does that even mean?

Annie shrugged.

What about the writer?

I don't know if there is a writer. There isn't a name attached. People are going crazy in Germany, trying to find out who's behind it. There are some theories, but I don't think any of them is particularly credible.

I heard it's twenty-four hours long, said Danny. A twenty-four-hour-long sex romp!

I doubt it's that long, Annie said. She looked across at Zara and rolled her eyes.

Yeah, but have you noticed they haven't announced the dates yet?

So?

So... There's something weird going on there. I mean, we all know it will start in a few weeks, after the end of *Death of a Saleswoman*, but I bet they're going to do something crazy. Like, I dunno, surprise the audience.

How do you surprise an audience? said Alessandra. Like a flash mob?

Well, I mean... isn't that the basics of good theatre? Zara said. Surprising the audience?

Someone's feeling philosophical, Danny said, tucking his cigarette behind his ear.

Who's directing again? asked Bembe.

Aimee Munro and Robbie Olufemi, Zara said. They're co-directing.

Co-directing! said Bembe, aghast. I have literally never heard of that happening in theatre. Especially by two household names!

Each of the productions has been co-directed, said Annie.

That's so random, said Danny.

It does happen, Alessandra said to Bembe. *SIX* was co-directed too.

It's not common, said Bembe. And *SIX* is a musical. That's different.

Alessandra shrugged and took a bite out of an apple.

That wasn't a dig at musical theatre, you know.

I know.

Okay, good, cos I do think it's a valuable art form, even though –

Bembe was interrupted by a rustling over the speaker. A hushed voice rang out: Five minutes till lights down, people, this is your five-minute interval call.

Uh oh, said Danny. That time already.

Annie, Bembe and Danny disappeared down the stairs to take up their positions in the foyer. Bembe was on the door, checking no one took glass into the auditorium; he offered plastic cups for audience members to decant their drinks into. Danny was selling programmes and playscripts. Annie was on cloakroom. The current production was Arthur Miller's American classic, *Death of a Salesman*, but with a female lead: something intended to update the script and give it a fresh, modern edge. The reviews were generally favourable; the production received the standard procession of four stars the theatre always achieved, with one critic writing that the production shone a light on the impossible pressures of being a woman in today's society. That one had made Zara laugh. What play written by a man about a man more than seventy years ago could shine a light on anything about being a woman today? Instead of staging an old play everyone had seen a million times, why not show something new? Also Casey Day, who played Wilhelmina Loman, wasn't any good. This was one of her first big jobs, so she was overly friendly with the bar staff and bought them drinks if she stayed late into the evening, but her performance was flat and made Zara cringe. She found herself wondering who Casey had had to fuck to get the part then told herself off for the unkind, unfeminist thought. It wasn't Casey's fault she was bad at acting. Casey regularly asked Zara and the other women actors if they'd had any auditions lately, something that might have been intended to bond them together as artists of the same craft and gender identity, to show she thought of herself as one of them, but which in practice resulted in Casey taking up a lot of their time with stories about her exciting auditions at the BBC or the National, weighing up the pros and cons of television work versus live theatre. They smiled politely whenever she talked but rolled their eyes behind her back and sometimes even did mean impressions, which Zara felt guilty about – but then, she hadn't heard from her agent in months and Alessandra's most recent job was as a dead girl in an anti-drink-driving campaign, so they felt a bit of meanness was justified.

Curtis peered around the corner. Zara, can you put the ice in your interval orders?

Yeah, she said. Already done.

Well, Curtis said, surveying the tables full of drinks with their little white slips. Remember not to do it too early, or else the ice will melt before the customers get to them. No one wants a watered-down gin and tonic, okay?

Okay, Zara said.

Alessandra scowled when Curtis left. We've only been working here for what? Three years? We know how to make interval orders, Curtis.

Hearing Alessandra casually refer to her three-year career as a front-of-house team member (first as an usher, then as a bartender) made Zara wince. This was supposed to be a temporary job, to fill the time before she went to drama school, but somehow the years had slipped by. Three years felt like forever. When she first took this job, she thought it would be for a few months, a year, tops, then, after she'd completed her MA, she would get enough acting work to move out of her mum's house. It seemed stupid, in retro-spect, to have been so sure, but she'd had to sell this future as a certainty to her mum to get her to co-sign the loan she needed for her drama school fees. On the way, she must have fallen for it herself too.

Customers began to trickle out of the auditorium, first in dribs and drabs, then a steady stream of them forming a queue at the bar. Alessandra and Zara bumped into each other, muttering 'oops' and 'sorry!' as they raced to fill glasses with champagne, squeeze wedges of lime into gin and tonics and pop the lids off bottles of beer. Finally, the five-minute call came over the speakers and the audience disappeared as quickly as they had arrived, until there were only a handful of people remaining. There was a guy stand-ing at the end of the bar by the cookies. Zara ignored him on purpose, hoping he would get the message and go back inside with the rest of the audience members.

Hi! Can I help you? Alessandra asked him. She was always cheery towards the customers – too cheery sometimes.

I'm just waiting to see if I can get your friend's attention, he said.

Zara fixed her eyes on the beer fridge, knowing that both Alessandra and the guy would be looking in her direction. She continued to count the beer bottles and made a note in the folder.

Alessandra dithered.

Erm, she said. She's kind of busy right now. Can I help you? You need to order quickly because the show will be starting again any second.

It's okay, the guy said. I'm not watching the show. I can wait.

Zara wanted Alessandra to tell him that he had to leave because this bar was closing now and that he could go to the bar downstairs, which would remain open after the show. That's what she would have said if the roles were reversed, not only to help out her friend but because it was true. But after a long pause Alessandra simply shrugged and continued to dry the clean glasses. Zara stood, wiping her hands on her jeans. The guy lit up as soon as she turned around. She noticed that his mouth was full of perfectly white, perfectly straight teeth. He slid down the bar towards her.

I was trying to play hard to get but I think I was playing too hard, he said. I'm James. He held out his hand. Zara shook it briefly, trying to convey her disdain with limited physical contact.

Hi James, she said. This bar is closing now, but the bar downstairs is still open.

Are you going to the bar downstairs?

No... I'm going to stay up here and help Alessandra close this bar.

Then can I stay up here with you and Alessandra? Just for a bit.

He grinned at Alessandra, who beamed back.

Zara folded her arms across her chest.

Why would you want to do that?

I just want to chat to you. Please?

But I'm working.

Will you meet me downstairs afterwards?

What? No. I don't know you.

But you could get to know me. James shrugged. He was playing at being apologetic, as though to say *hey, can you blame a guy for trying?* This faux sweetness put the onus on Zara to respond in a particular way. In the real world, outside the restrictions of employment, she would tell him to get lost, but here, in her customer service role, she had to be nice and polite. Otherwise, Curtis would tell her off for being rude to customers (again). James knew the score. He was using it to his advantage.

I'm sorry, she said. I've got somewhere to be after work, so I can't.

Hey, no worries. Another time, maybe?

Zara heard Curtis's voice on the stairs. She was trying to figure out the politest way to say no, not another time, please leave me alone for real, when James slipped her a scrap of paper over the bar and walked away, towards the stairs. He passed Curtis on the way, and they acknowledged each other with an 'all right', as though they were friends.

He seemed nice, Alessandra said, peering over Zara's shoulder to look at the piece of paper James had given her.

It was a receipt from Pret, for a tuna cheese toasted sandwich and a can of fizzy ginger. On the back, in a childish scrawl, it said *JAMES*, followed by a phone number.

So annoying, Zara said, stuffing the scrap into the back pocket of her jeans.

Really?

Yeah, like, I'm at work?

Alessandra shrugged and began to reload the glasswasher.

How's it going up here? said Curtis. He winked at Zara. I see someone's getting 'intimate' with our new leading man.

Sorry?

James. He's the lead in… *Intimacy*, said Curtis, doing jazz hands.

She rejected him.

Really? Huh. I think he's pretty hot. I heard he had a thing with Casey Day, once upon a time.

Not my type, said Zara.

Suit yourself. So, which of you girls is going to count the cash?

Zara didn't have anywhere special to go after work. She had been planning on staying for a drink with Bembe and Danny, but the situation with James had put her in an irritable mood. She decided to go home. So he was going to be hanging around for a while. So she was going to have to put up with him lurking around the bar, bugging her for the next few months. Great. On the bus, she searched the internet for *James. Actor. Intimacy. London.* but nothing came up. The cast hadn't been announced yet. She ran a search for *James. Actor. London.* but there were way too many hits. She closed her eyes and tried to remember what he looked like. He did have a cute smile, if maybe a little *too* dazzling (did he whiten his teeth?), and to be fair to him, he did have kind eyes. There was something about him that completely turned her off, but she wasn't sure what. Maybe she was so disillusioned with her job that the most generous, sweet, lovely, attractive man in the world could try to chat her up and she would miss him altogether.

Bembe found out about the number-giving incident and messaged her:

TEXT HIM.
IMMEDIATELY.
NOW.
OR I WILL NEVER FORGIVE YOU.

> *What?? This is such a bad idea!!*
> *The actor in the show?!*

Babe, you've been telling me for months that
you want to go on a date with a nice guy. I
saw him in the bar. He introduced himself to me
a lowly usher. He seems like a nice guy. Nicer
than any of the other guys you normally date
I put up with you moaning on and on about them
even though I could have told you from one look

at their Bumble profile that they were bad news
So you should do this. For me

Right... you know that whole
message is incredibly problematic??

Not everything needs to be analysed, Z
Sometimes it can just be fun

Back home, in her bedroom, Zara took the receipt out of her pocket and looked at it again. It would be awkward if things went badly. Both of them working in the same theatre, him coming down to the bar for post-show drinks and her having to serve him his gin and tonic, trying to avoid making eye contact. That awkwardness hadn't stopped her from sleeping with Nick, an usher who had worked at the theatre for a little while before he left to do a schools tour. But it would be different with an actor in the show. No one cared about Nick.

Zara fell asleep and dreamed she lost the receipt. Her room was a tip. Clothes, clean and dirty, in among books, scraps of paper, candles, make-up, crisp packets, balls of hair and dirt, chewing gum, all piled up in mounds all over the floor. She could hardly see the carpet. When she opened her wardrobe or drawers, more of these piles of miscellaneous items spilled out, objects slipping and sliding over each other like coins in the penny machines she'd played as a kid. Everything moving, as though it was alive, mixed together in such a way that it was impossible to locate the receipt anywhere. She dived into the piles, searching through bras and old necklaces, chasing anything that looked like a little white slip, until there was no room to move, the objects were pushing into her, up around her face, and there was hardly any room to breathe –

She woke to the sound of her phone vibrating on the table next to her, a grumpy clicking sound like a trapped insect. She grabbed the phone and, in her disoriented state, didn't check to see who was calling before answering.

Hello?

Zara, it's Candice. Are you all right?

The voice was perky, high-pitched, unfamiliar. Zara cleared her throat. Yes, I'm fine, thanks. And you?

Oh yes, I'm great. It's just… You sound like you've only just woken up and it's ten o'clock in the morning! You aren't *ill*, are you?

The combination of her sleepiness and the fact that it had been so long since Zara had spoken to her agent on the telephone meant it took her a second to remember who Candice was. But Candice's trademark passive-aggressive criticism reminded her with a bright snap of shame.

No… No, no. Not at all. I feel good actually. Healthy, you know?

Zara heard traffic sounds in the background and the long inhalation that meant Candice was smoking a cigarette.

Well, that's fantastic. Because you've got an audition.

I have?

You have indeed, and it's a big one. At the Baylis. I'm sure you've been there before. It's for their upcoming production of *Intimacy*. Have you heard of it? It's a two-hander, new writing from Germany. It's been a big hit, you know, in Germany and New York, and now it's coming to London. It's interpretive, immersive, really cutting-edge. Exciting, right? The audition is today, at 2 p.m. I've already confirmed everything, so if you just go to stage door for about ten to two, to make a good impression, they should be expecting you. I think that's all. Any questions?

Wow. I don't know what to say. I mean, how did you get me this audition?

Well... Candice made a sound halfway between a laugh and a cough. Well, I didn't exactly put you up for it myself... The brief was vague. I mean like, super vague. Nobody knew what they wanted... But this is an incredible opportunity for you, Zara. You should go for it!

So, if you didn't put me up for it... Did they ask for me?

Uh, yes. They did. Zara Bright. That's you, right? Candice barked out a laugh. Zara heard her take another drag of her cigarette.

Yes, but... I work at the Baylis.

So? What's the problem? Maybe somebody saw you there and decided you'd be just right for it. I don't know. But don't overthink it. I have to go. But you'll go, right? You'll do the audition? The casting director is a big deal. I don't think we should let him down. And this is a truly amazing opportunity for you, Zara. Once in a lifetime really –

Yes, yes. Of course I will. Of course. Thank you, Candice. Thank you so much.

Candice had already hung up the phone. Zara opened her laptop and checked through her emails, scanning for the audition confirmation, almost willing it not to be there. But it popped into her inbox, right in front of her eyes. The most she ever hoped for when she got an email from Candice (because they rarely spoke on the phone) was a cattle call for an advert or maybe an audition for a small part in a regional fringe theatre production, if she was lucky. But then she remembered James. He was the only other performer in *Intimacy*, if the gossip was to be believed, and he'd given her his number yesterday, and now all of a sudden, she, Zara, a nobody in the acting world, had an audition at the Baylis, of all the theatres in London. Zara checked the email again, and the original email had been sent by a casting director, one she had heard of. She double-checked the email address. It all seemed legit, but still.

Zara opened the door to her mum's bedroom. It was dark inside. Her mum was a midwife – she'd been working nights this week, but she wouldn't mind being woken up for this.

Mum?

Zara? Is everything okay? Her mum bolted upright, eye mask tangled in her hair.

Yeah, yeah. Everything's fine. Can I talk to you about something quickly?

Well, I'm awake now. I suppose you may as well.

It's just… Something weird happened to me.

Mm?

Zara caught her up on the whole situation, from James chatting her up at the bar, his number, the audition, even the dream. Her mum stayed silent throughout, looking down at her floral duvet cover.

So what do you think I should do?

Zara's mum sighed and rubbed her eyes. So, let me get this straight. You got asked on a date by an attractive man, a successful actor, who might be a little bit cheesy. And now you've got the most exciting audition of your career thus far. What do you need help with exactly? Her mum's eyes were small and sleepy, her hands folded in her lap.

But... Isn't it weird?

I suppose so. Her mum reached for a glass of water on her bedside table. But good things come in threes, don't they? I'm sure this is your lucky streak, sweetheart.

But what if they're only auditioning me because James fancies me?

He's not famous, is he? He's just an ordinary actor. Why would they audition you just because he asked?

I'm worried it might not be a real audition though.

But you told me you saw the email from the casting director. You checked the email address. Don't get so worried about all these details. Focus your energies on the audition! And maybe afterwards you should think about going on that date...

Yeah, thanks a lot.

Right. I'm working again tonight. I need my beauty sleep. But good luck, darling! Let me know how it goes.

When Zara exited Waterloo Tube station three hours later, she still had doubts. She'd prepared as if the audition was real. Showered carefully, put on the perfect minimal make-up and brushed her teeth multiple times. She did a bit of yoga, some vocal warm-ups. She looked herself in the eye before she left and said aloud, You got this. You can do anything you put your mind to. The streets were heaving with the typical Saturday afternoon mix of tourists and day trippers. People with sensible shoes, bags with lots of zippable pockets and adjustable straps. There were kids screaming, either in joy or pain, it was difficult to tell. The odd homeless person also joining in the merriment by screaming back, much to the panic of the children's parents. Pigeons squawked and shat. The air stank of fumes, dirt and cigarette smoke. It made her feel a bit more normal.

She walked to the stage door. The matinee performance of *Death of a Saleswoman* was about to start. All the theatre staff should be in their places. It was important to Zara that no one here knew she'd had an audition, as though speaking about it would interrupt the manifestation process. The only person she couldn't avoid was the stage door manager, Albert.

Zara! he said, buzzing her in. You look nice. Aren't you late?

Am I? What time was I supposed to be here?

She could feel tiny pinpricks of sweat breaking out of her armpits, across the skin of her upper lip.

Don't the shifts start at one any more? Or are you not working till tonight?

What? No. I'm not here to work. I've got a... I've got an audition. For *Intimacy*? My agent called me this morning, so...

Well, Albert said, flicking through the various pieces of paper littered around his desk. No one's told me anything about that, I'm afraid. I'll call up to the rehearsal room though. I think the *Intimacy* team are up there right now.

There haven't been any other auditions today?

Nope. They held quite a few auditions a month or so ago. Nothing since then. Don't worry though, love. We'll get to the bottom of this.

Albert winked at her, and Zara thought she saw a flicker of pity in his eyes. Oh god. Her heart was chomping in her chest like a horse about to break out of the gate. She could feel sweat needling her back and her neck, her face and underarms. Was she beginning to smell too? Zara checked the time on her phone and flipped the camera to selfie mode. She smiled down at herself. She would get her face prepared. At this point, she couldn't stop herself from being humiliated, but she would endure it with grace.

The stage door manager reappeared.

Good news! They are expecting you. Bad news, though, is that they can't find the other actor.

What other actor?

James something. Haven't you met him? He's been hanging around the building for a few days. He was supposed to read with you. They've asked if you can hang on for a couple more minutes while they try to… locate him.

Oh yeah. That's fine. No problem.

Behind him, the phone began to ring. Excuse me, Albert said.

James. Of course. Zara clasped her hands together and

tried to steady her breathing. She would not pick the varnish off her freshly painted nails. She was so close; she would not lose it.

Albert hung up the phone and peered out at her. Zara beamed back at him. He gave her a half-hearted smile and returned to his papers. After a few minutes, the phone rang again. Zara tried to make out what Albert was saying, but he kept his voice low, his eyes darting occasionally in her direction.

All right, Albert said after a while. Showtime! They're going to see you on your own, without James. You can go up to the rehearsal room. You know where it is, don't you? They're waiting for you.

The rehearsal room was at the top of the building. There were several floors, and a staircase that wound round and around and around. By the time she got to the top, Zara was out of breath and a bit dizzy. She stopped to compose herself, but there was a team of people waiting in front of the rehearsal room door. One of them was wearing a headset and holding a clipboard.

Zara Bright?

Yes, that's me.

Go on through.

Zara stepped through the door, and someone closed it firmly behind her. Her eyes adjusted to the dim light. There, in the centre of the room, a narrow spot of orange light. The skylights, which usually made this the brightest room in the building, had been covered over with heavy black fabric.

Come forward, a voice called. Into the light.

Zara moved towards the single beam. The figure of a man emerged from the gloom. He was wearing thick glasses and a pink flowery shirt. Beside him, a woman in a cream silk blouse stared at her laptop screen. Zara stepped gingerly into the glow of the light. She felt like she was about to stand trial or be beamed up into a spaceship.

Hello, she said.

You can begin, the man said.

Is there... Zara cleared her throat. Is there something in particular you'd like me to read?

Hadn't Candice said there would be a script? Something for her to sight-read? She couldn't remember now. She ought to have clarified.

You should have something prepared, the woman intoned. Any monologue will do.

Zara's mind had gone completely blank. After a brief hesitation, she began a short *Alice in Wonderland* monologue, one she'd learned by heart in the first year of secondary school. The words unspooled from her as though they were written inside her body.

I believe I have been falling for five minutes, and I still can't see the bottom! Hmph! After such a fall as this, I shall think nothing of tumbling downstairs. How brave they'll all think me at home...

The man frowned a little. The woman's face did not move. Zara knew it wasn't what they wanted, but she had nothing else.

Can you sing and dance at the same time?

Zara nodded.

The woman watched Zara expectantly. Well... Could you?

Zara laughed, but neither the man nor the woman moved.

But there isn't any music.

Oh, said the woman, clacking out a note on her laptop. Is that a problem?

No, no. Of course not.

The woman raised her eyebrow and waited. It was difficult to make out their faces clearly in the glare of the lights. Maybe she was imagining their impatient, frustrated expressions. She told herself to think good thoughts. Maybe they were pleasantly surprised by what she was doing. Maybe they loved her. The room was silent except for the angry buzz of the light, the occasional rustle of the casting director's papers. Zara began to sing 'Can't Get You Out of My Head' by Kylie Minogue. She danced as though she was in a nightclub, shaking her shoulders and flipping her hair. Towards the end, she started pirouetting and then, for some inexplicable reason, dropped to her knees and tossed her head from side to side. When the song was over, she got to her feet in silence.

All right then, said the woman. We need you to remove your clothes. You can keep your underwear on.

Here? Now?

Yes, now. That's not a problem, is it?

The assistant stepped out from behind her desk. Zara could see she was wearing a tight-fitting pencil skirt and black patent heels. A tape measure dangled from her fingers.

Just standard measurements, that's all.

Zara peered around the room, into the dark corners, as though there might be someone else, someone hiding, someone who might laugh so she could too, but there was no such person. Zara did as she was told. She was wearing an old pair of knickers, which had smiley face emojis printed all over them. Once they had been a pale lilac colour; now they were bobbly and discoloured, the lace trim unravelling in places. Her lucky knickers. Her bra was newish, so that was something. Black satin. The man's eyes moved over the bra, across Zara's belly, her thighs, down to her feet. There were a few flecks of red on her toenails. They needed a trim. The casting director nodded at the assistant, and she held her tape aloft to measure Zara's height. Then she wrapped the tape around Zara's waist, her head, each thigh. Zara began to feel cold. She crossed her arms over her chest, but the assistant moved them back to her sides. The assistant asked Zara to confirm what she had eaten for breakfast. Zara remembered the cheese and bacon pastries she had bought from Pret on her way in – not one, but two – and the oat flat white. She'd bought a Twix too, but that was still in her bag. She thought of it longingly. She would get herself a cup of tea after this. She deserved one. The assistant was waiting.

Oh right, Zara said. Sorry. Um, I had a bowl of granola, I think. Yeah, that was it. And an apple. And a… a black coffee.

The assistant raised her eyebrows at her laptop screen. Thank you for your time.

That's it? I can go?

Yes, the assistant said, without looking up from her screen. You can go.

Zara noticed that the casting director had disappeared from the room. She got dressed quickly and thanked the assistant again. The assistant did not respond.

The people who had been waiting outside, with their clipboards and radios, had all gone. Zara made her way straight into the top-floor bathroom. It was empty. Natural light flooded in through the skylight and made everything glow. Outside, the day had turned bright and beautiful. Zara looked at herself in the mirror. She leaned in close to examine the tiny flecks of yellow in her eyes, the smattering of freckles on the bridge of her nose. She turned her attention to her pupils, those spots of black at the centre of her eyes, and she recoiled. You smashed it, babe, she thought, but did not say it aloud.

Zara didn't go back to the theatre for a few days, not because she was avoiding it but because she wasn't rota'd onto any shifts. She lay on the sofa and watched eight episodes of *Emily in Paris* back to back. Alone in her room, the audition began to feel distant and surreal, like a scene from a strange movie. Sometimes she found herself wondering if it had happened at all. But no – it had happened. She knew it had. She had been there, in the room. But still, her mum, the only person Zara had told, hadn't mentioned it since.

Even Candice, who had a financial interest in the success of the audition, hadn't checked in. Zara wondered if the casting director had been in touch with her directly, to express his disappointment. Twice she had logged out of her inbox and back in, to check it was sending and receiving properly. She emailed herself and the message arrived instantly, a gleaming, defiant test.

.   .   .

Did you hear? Alessandra asked as she chopped lemons and limes for service. Annie had an audition for *Intimacy*.

Really? Zara tried to keep her expression impassive. It was her first shift back after her audition, and she still hadn't told anyone about it.

Yeah, she got a call out of the blue. Her agent knows the casting director apparently.

That's... Wow. That's so crazy.

Her audition was on Monday, Alessandra continued. She thinks it went well. Imagine if she gets the part!

Imagine! Zara giggled, but it came out wrong, too high-pitched. She arranged the snacks in the display basket to give herself something to do with her hands. She dropped one packet, then another. I think we need more cookies, she said.

Okay, Alessandra said dreamily, brushing the hair out of her eyes. She grabbed another fat lemon from her pile and sliced it clean in half.

Zara held on to the banister as she walked downstairs. She tried to ignore the fluttering, scraping feeling inside her chest. Something about the fact Annie had had an audition unsettled her, but what was it? The memory of her own audition? Jealousy? Or the brutal realization that she was not the only one, that she had not been lucky or special to get the audition, that she was one of many girls they would see? But then they would see more than one person. She just didn't think it would be Annie. She had even less acting experience than Zara. In fact, hadn't Annie said she was thinking of quitting acting? She was sick of performing in tiny theatres above pubs for no pay, just for the opportunity. She was tired of playing small roles which ended in boring death or meaningless suffering to fulfil another character's arc. She was thinking of directing instead, that's what she'd said. Then something else occurred to Zara: had James shown up for Annie's audition? What if that had given her the edge?

She emerged from the stockroom, arms full of cookies. Her mind was whirring. It probably didn't mean anything, she told herself. Why would they have bothered auditioning her at all if the lack of James was a deal-breaker? She didn't notice Bembe approaching until he was at her elbow.

Oh my god, she said. You scared me.

Bembe gave her a strange look. You okay babe?

Yeah, sorry. I was just surprised to see you.

Okay... And where have you been?

Nowhere special. I just didn't have any shifts.

Have you heard the goss?

What, about Annie?

Oh, you mean her date with James?

Wait, what? Annie went on a date with *James*?

Yeah, last Saturday night. But that's old news now. No – you heard about Alessandra?

What about Alessandra?

She's got an audition for *Intimacy* too!

Are you serious? I'm on the bar with her. She didn't say anything.

It literally just came in. I was up there as she was getting off the phone. Her audition is tomorrow morning.

What? I… Wow.

And the other news is that Annie is going on another date with James. Tomorrow night.

Zara made a sound, but the words stuck in her throat.

I know right, Bembe continued. I think she thinks it'll help her land the part. To be fair, you can see the logic. If it comes down to that – you know, which girl has the best chemistry with him – then it's a strong tactic. But at the same time, would they want to take the risk? I mean, if you were a director of a play like this, all about feelings and whatever, would you want your leads mixed up with each other? What if their little fling goes badly? Personally, I wouldn't get into anything with a co-performer. Anyway, Annie was absolutely convinced she'd got the role. She's going to freak when she hears Alessandra's got an audition.

Someone called Bembe's name. They both turned. It was the front-of-house manager, gesturing with exasperation towards the cloakroom.

Oh. Right, Bembe said. Better keep an eye on your phone, Z. At this rate, they'll be calling you in too.

He grinned at Zara as he walked away.

Her heart was louder now, panic simmering through her body. She rounded the corner and almost collided with Curtis. And just behind him, James.

Woah. Zara, what are you doing down here? Curtis said. We're going to open upstairs in less than five minutes.

Zara hesitated. James winked at her over Curtis's shoulder. She wanted to leave, get out of here. A feeling bordering on urgency. She could say she had a headache. Maybe period pains. Or a mental health crisis. Whatever would make Curtis most uncomfortable. But then she knew this feeling was irrational. Nothing had changed, not really. No one knew she had been called in for an audition first, and if she didn't get the part, no one would ever know. What did it matter if Annie got the part? Or Alessandra? Wouldn't that be a good thing? Wouldn't that be something to celebrate? And besides, there was James. His eyes on her. Hovering behind Curtis, listening. She didn't want to show any weakness.

Hello? Zara?

I was getting the cookies, she said, jigging the packages in her arms. We were nearly out.

Right, well. Hurry along, okay? Curtis said. It's not fair to leave Alessandra up there on her own.

The show was sold out, as usual, and the incoming was hectic. The water dispenser kept being drained. As soon as it was empty, customers would gather round, take it in turns to tilt it this way and that, then shake their heads and stare pointedly in the direction of the bar until one of the girls rushed to fill it for them. They were short-staffed that night, so once the show started, Alessandra was moved to an ushering position inside the auditorium. She waved goodbye to Zara. They hadn't had a chance to talk yet, but Zara noticed a small, private smile of self-satisfaction which lit up Alessandra's face from within. Zara cleaned up and prepared for the interval on her own. She kept spilling things: miscalculating the distance between her hand and the edge of the bar, the speed at which to pour a single glass of wine into a flimsy plastic cup. What was wrong with her? She was jittery, as though she was about to be found out for something bad she had done. But she hadn't done anything wrong. She didn't owe anyone the information about her own audition. It was her right to keep it quiet, keep it safe.

Throughout the shift, names were traded among the front-of-house team, whispered in the darkness of the voms or the stale air of the changing rooms. Names of girls who worked at the theatre, the girls who had recently left, those they hadn't heard from in a while. Friends of friends. Peers from drama schools. Ex-castmates. Zara imagined them all, a long line of them, girls just like her, their faces hesitant but excited before they entered that dark room on the top floor.

After they clocked out, Alessandra asked Zara to stay for a drink. Danny was working a late shift on the bar with Curtis. There was a new cocktail menu, so Curtis was showing Danny how to make each new cocktail. Then he passed the spares across the bar. They discussed Alessandra's audition, and Zara dredged up enthusiasm from reserves she didn't know she had. Other members of staff joined them, and the story was repeated. The wattage on Zara's performance turned up as high as it would go, so high she thought cracks were beginning to appear. But no one was looking at her; no one noticed. It was quiet, a typical weekday evening. Other than the front-of-house staff, there were only a handful of customers. Some had been to see the show that evening, but most were regulars – those who lived nearby, or perhaps those who had nowhere else to go. They were at least three drinks down when Casey Day walked in.

Oh look, said Bembe, giving Zara a nudge. It's your bestie.

Shut up.

What? Annie asked, aghast. You don't like her?

No! I mean, yes. I do like her. Of course I do.

She's so lovely!

Yes, she is, Zara said.

Alessandra caught Zara's eye and smirked.

What? Annie said again. I feel like you're all keeping something from me. What is it?

Don't be silly, Annie.

Zara turned in her chair to look at Casey. She waved and pulled a face. She was surrounded by a gaggle of adoring fans, wanting selfies and autographs. Danny pushed a Blue Lagoon across the bar and Zara snatched it up.

Hey, it was definitely my turn, said Bembe. You already had one of those.

Oh... Did I? Whoops. Zara gave him a sarcastic smile. Touché.

Casey finally made her way over. She clutched a bottle of Evian in her hand. Her face was shiny, but not with sweat, with some sort of cream. Probably an expensive one. She looked healthy and young. Not youthful – young, like a child before puberty hits. Casey had big news.

I've got an audition for *Intimacy*! I'm so excited, she gushed. I just love new writing. It's the most exciting part of theatre.

Wow, said Bembe. Congratulations.

Everyone else murmured their congratulations, but the atmosphere was strained. Of course Casey of all people would have an audition. Of course. It made sense. But the number of auditionees was becoming unsettling, especially to those who had thought they were in with a chance. Annie looked stricken. The corners of Bembe's lips flickered. His eyes were bright. Zara knew what was coming. He couldn't resist the opportunity to stir the pot.

Is it tomorrow? Your audition? Bembe said. Alessandra glared at him and shook her head slightly, but he pretended not to notice.

No, it's on Friday, Casey said, still beaming.

Ah, that's a shame. You'll miss Alessandra.

Casey's smile faltered. I'm sorry?

Her audition for *Intimacy* is tomorrow. Isn't it, Alessandra?

Yes, Alessandra said, nodding. I have an audition tomorrow.

For *Intimacy*? Casey said.

Yep.

There was a long pause. Annie looked like she was about to burst into tears or wet herself. I had one too, she said, the words tumbling, almost unintelligible. It was on Monday. I don't even know why I got one. I guess my agent knows the casting director or something? I probably won't get the part anyway. The audition was super weird. Who knows? But yeah. I had one too.

Casey surveyed them all. She scrutinized their expressions carefully, as though she could catch them out for lying, as though she was caught up in a prank for a hidden camera show. She waited, but Ashton Kutcher did not appear. She was not being punk'd. Well, congratulations all! she said eventually. What an exciting day! Let's raise our glasses to *Intimacy* – and to the Baylis girls! Hopefully one of us will get the part.

Everyone raised their glasses, their half-drunk cocktails, and clinked them obediently. Zara fixed her gaze on the wall behind Casey's head and smiled. She could feel Bembe looking at her, trying to catch her eye.

The next week was the last of the run and, unusually, the front-of-house team hadn't been told how long the theatre would be dark.

I can't believe they still haven't told us when *Intimacy* is opening, Bembe said. What are people supposed to do if it's gonna be like, three months off? At least I've got my cafe job twice a week, but that's not enough on its own.

Mm, I know, Zara said. Bloody zero-hours contracts. Times like this, I'm glad I still live with my mum.

It could be ages. They still haven't cast the other actor. And you'd have thought they'd be well into rehearsals by now, wouldn't you?

Zara murmured in agreement. They were sitting on a bench on the South Bank. They had been to see a rerun of *Mulholland Drive* at the BFI. Zara had seen it before; she didn't get it either time, but Bembe insisted that was the whole point of the film, its inscrutability. There was no sense to be made out of it. It was all vibes. The sunshine was thin and watery through the clouds, the breeze bitter. Zara had goosebumps on her arms. They had just heard that Annie had been recalled for a second audition. It seemed her first had gone well. Better than Zara's anyway: she still hadn't heard anything.

What is James doing at the theatre every day anyway? Bembe said. He can't be rehearsing a two-hander alone.

Maybe someone's reading in for her until the part is cast, Zara said.

Well... Who says it's a her? Bembe said. Maybe they're getting another guy this time.

Yeah, but we know they've mainly auditioned women.

Do we? Bembe waggled his eyebrows.

Wait – you haven't?

Bembe froze, as though caught out. Wide eyes, hand raised to his mouth. Then he erupted with laughter. Course I haven't, he said. You should have seen your face!

During the dark period, Zara tried to think about other things. She turned her mind to self-improvement. She committed to a skincare regime morning and evening. She looked up advanced acting courses and considered asking her mum for the money to enrol. She wanted to try out Meisner, or perhaps clowning. Something to shake up her technique, to get her unstuck. One of the ushers at work had been to Lecoq, and never shut up about the school's methods. That same girl had since taken a long-term role at an immersive theatre production in West London, so it had worked out for her. Zara started a thirty-day yoga programme on YouTube. She forced herself to read some of the playscripts she had stacked on her bedside table, the ones she'd been meaning to read but had never got around to. *Woyzeck, Hedda Gabler, Rosencrantz and Guildenstern Are Dead.*

·   ·   ·

Zara's phone rang just after lunch. She was sitting on the balcony, in the shade, watching the neighbourhood children squeal at each other in the street below – they were having a water fight. She looked at her phone. It was Candice.

They want you, Candice said, without a word of greeting. They want you for a chemistry read.

A what?

A chemistry read. You've been pencilled!

It took Zara a few seconds to understand what was going on. She had been studiously avoiding thinking too much about *Intimacy*, and Candice's words were unfamiliar, an entirely different language. Her voice sounded different too. Was that delight? A genuine laugh?

I've been pencilled?

Yes, for *Intimacy*. You don't have the part nailed down just yet, but it's getting close!

Oh my god, Zara said. That's amazing. And what does it mean, the... uh?

The chemistry read, right. They want to suss out whether there's anything between you and James. The leading man. You met him in the audition, right?

Well, no. He wasn't there actually. But I have met him.

Fantastic. The directors and the creator will be there this time. They want to see you together – they want to see sparks fly. Can you do that for me?

Zara hesitated. She could act. That was what she'd been trained to do. That was what she knew how to do. She could fake chemistry; that wouldn't be a problem, would it?

Zara? You can make the magic happen, right?

The magic.

Of course I can, Zara said.

This is quite the opportunity, Zara! Candice said, again and again. Quite the opportunity.

While Candice was speaking, Zara continued to observe the children in the street. The midday sun was so fierce their bodies had begun to shimmer, their outlines distorted, hazy in the heat. As she watched, shadow and child blurred, taking on ever more strange and grotesque shapes. Zara opened her mouth to – what? Scream? Tell Candice what she could see? But nothing came out.

Just then, a bus rolled past. On its side, an outdated advert for *Death of a Saleswoman*, Casey Day beaming in a pristine, bubblegum-pink suit, a glass of champagne held aloft. Everything snapped back into focus: the bus moved on and the children reappeared, back in their bodies, as though nothing had happened.

Zara went upstairs to look at herself in the bathroom mirror.

I will get this part, she said aloud. I deserve this part.

She read more about manifestation and the law of attraction, as though she had any control over the situation. She told herself out loud that the part was hers. This was a formality. *She had the part.* She would be on the stage of the Baylis. Her face would appear on the sides of buses. People would know her name. She would gaze at herself in the dressing room mirror, the one Casey Day had used.

Once Zara had lingered in the corridor outside while Casey was getting ready for that night's performance. Her face was luminous, ethereal, framed in lights. On the table in front of her, a large, purple bottle of Listerine, a brand-new toothbrush still in its packet, shiny tubes of lipstick and dusty cases of powder, blusher and eyeshadow, all half-used and mixed up, the colours indistinct. Zara watched from the shadows while Casey patted her face, spritzed it down, swept a large brush across it. She turned this way and that, examining her face from every angle. When she was done, she stared at herself for a long time, before inexplicably exploding with laughter.

The theatre's website said *Intimacy* was sold out. How could it be sold out already? Zara wasn't even aware tickets had gone on sale yet. She must have missed the announcement. Apparently it was pencilled for a 'very limited' run. Tickets would be allocated to audience members who'd signed up to a ballot weeks ago. They would be assigned a date and time at random. No one got to choose. It all sounded unnecessarily complicated, very cloak-and-dagger. Zara supposed it was marketing: a ploy to create intrigue and demand. She would have to ask someone from box office to sneak her mum in.

Zara wanted to talk to her mum, but she was always at the hospital. She was on day shifts now, leaving the house hours before Zara even woke up. The phone rang and rang. With each ring, Zara became more and more uncertain that talking to her about this was the best idea. How would she explain 'chemistry read' and 'pencil'? What if voicing it somehow jinxed it and she didn't get the part? What if her mum didn't say 'break a leg' but said 'good luck' instead? That was exactly the kind of thing she would do without thinking – and Zara shouldn't even have the words 'good luck' floating around in her head at all. She hung up. When her mum finally called back, hours later, Zara turned her phone face down and waited for the call to ring out.

The chemistry read was at five the next day. Zara went straight to stage door. Albert was there. He greeted her like usual, but he couldn't look her in the eye.

Yes, he said. Of course. I know they're expecting you this time. Congratulations, Zara. Enjoy your moment on the big stage!

Zara thanked him and made her way up the winding staircase. Something about what Albert said unsettled her. *Enjoy your moment on the big stage.* She had assumed the chemistry read would be in the rehearsal room, like the audition. In her visualizations, when everything had gone well, it had taken place there. Would she be able to transpose that good energy to the main stage? And why should it be on the main stage anyway? Maybe they wanted to stage-test her, to see if she had enough gravitas for all that space. But there was something else too, the way he said *your moment* as though she was a child with a role in the school nativity, a brief stint in the spotlight before the baton was passed on to someone else. It didn't sit right with her. This was supposed to be the start, the lightning moment for a long, remarkable career, not *the* moment.

It was quiet backstage, almost eerie. Sunlight fell through the windows in clean, bright stripes. One of the stage management team intercepted her on the stairs.

Zara! she said, taking her by the elbow. How lovely to see you. I'm Camille. Let's go in here for a sec.

They ducked into an office at the top of the stairs. There were no lights on. The desks were empty, the computers silent. Zara noticed the bins had been emptied.

Before we go in for the read, I want to talk to you about the process. *Intimacy* isn't like other plays, and so at every stage we have to take a somewhat... unconventional approach.

Zara nodded. Her throat was dry. The quiet in the room felt sticky, almost oppressive.

We want to jump right in with an improvisation exercise, to get you warmed up. Throw you in at the deep end, so to speak. Do you think you'll be okay with that? The premise of the show is that James is your possessive lover. But we don't want to get bogged down in details. You can make the role your own.

It's a fluid process, Camille continued. Very instinctive. We want to see how you respond to certain stimuli on the stage. Is that all right? James has been working on some scenes today – he's very much in role – so we're going to go straight into it and do all the admin and introductions afterwards. We want you to play alongside him and see what comes out. It might feel uncomfortable or unfamiliar at first, but I think you can handle it. Don't you? And of course we have a mental health team on board. They're around somewhere, and they'll definitely be around after the performance, should you wish to speak to someone. We want to ensure you feel supported. Does all that sound okay? Right. Camille checked her watch. All right. It's about time. Any questions before we head in?

They reached the door that led to the stage. A sign above their heads read PERFORMANCE IN PROGRESS. Camille opened the door and pushed Zara into the wings.

She looked across the blank, harshly lit space of the stage. James was lurking opposite, doing up the buttons on his shirt. He winked at her, and she realized she couldn't do it. No – all the wanting, all the wishing, the visualizations, it was all for nothing. Something bad would happen if she stayed. She could feel it in her bones.

Camille was between Zara and the door.

It's all right, Zara. Trust me. It's you they're waiting for.

Please, I don't think I want to.

This will all make sense soon.

What do you mean?

Don't overthink it. Just go.

James ambled onstage. The lights hit his face. There was a rustling sound, a slight cough from someone in the auditorium, a collective intake of breath.

This is your chance, Camille said. Take it. She gave Zara's hand a quick squeeze, then pushed her gently in the direction of the stage. Zara took a deep breath, then stepped out of the darkness and into the light.

The first thing she noticed was the audience. The theatre was packed. It turned out that the audience did not become invisible in the glare of stage lights like people said. Zara could tell the auditorium was filled with people. Hundreds of them. She squinted, her eyes adjusting. The next thing she noticed was James's expression. Hard, unmoving. Acting, she told herself. He was only acting.

Oh, look who it is, he said. So you've decided to come back?

Zara froze. Her arms were clasped around her body, as though she was bracing for an attack. She looked around wildly. What was she supposed to say? She hoped to see a familiar face, a friendly face – Camille perhaps, or a director, even an usher – but there was nothing. No one and everyone all at once.

What's the matter? James snarled. Cat got your tongue?

Someone in the audience sniggered. This was supposed to be a chemistry read. Where was the chemistry? Zara thought of all the definitions she'd read: a spark between people, an energetic connection, intense attraction, effortless affection. She could do it, couldn't she? She could fake it.

Zara started to say something, but the words were muted and wobbly. Her body was shaking; she'd lost control. James crossed the stage behind her.

SPEAK. UP. He bellowed the words and Zara flinched then burst into tears.

Pathetic, he said, as he walked away. What did I tell you? He spoke to the audience. This is what I have to deal with.

Time out, Zara whispered. Time out, she said again, a little louder.

Time out? James said. Oh yes, time out. He looked around into the audience. Time out? That's all right, isn't it? We'll just stop here for today and get her a cup of tea. Is that right?

The audience laughed, a few more of them this time.

It's not over until I say it's over, James said. You owe me some answers.

Zara stood up and tried to leave the stage. There was someone from stage management in the wings, blocking the exit.

I can't let you out, he whispered. I'm sorry.

I need to talk to Camille, Zara whispered back. I need to start again.

You're doing great, the guy from stage management said. Don't give up now.

Zara closed her eyes.

Tick-tock, James said from his position onstage. I'm waiting!

The hour onstage was the longest of Zara's life. She stopped thinking about the performance, the sparks, and focused on holding it together, surviving James's onslaught. But about halfway through, the knot in the pit of her stomach began to loosen a little. She was onstage, and she'd survived so far. The audience began to feel less terrifying, and James's words rolled off her. She had become immune to them. She could handle them. His face, in which she had seen such dizzying contempt, was ridiculous. Laughable really. You could get used to anything, she realized. If you gave it long enough.

What do you want from me? Zara screamed at the denouement. Or what felt like the denouement, anyway.

James backed away from her and disappeared into the wings. She was left alone on the stage. A minute of pure brilliance – Zara had it all to herself.

I'm not your plaything, she yelled. You need to let me go, for both our sakes.

The lights faded to black. A silent second, then the audience thundered. Zara brushed her hair out of her eyes and looked around. She couldn't see a thing. Someone grabbed her by the wrist. This way, they purred into her ear.

Zara was led away from the audience, away from the clapping and cheering, her celebration. She found herself back in the office, opposite Camille. She couldn't hear the audience any more; it was almost as though they'd never been there at all.

Zara! Camille said, opening her arms for a hug. You did a great job!

Zara's body began to shake violently then, out of sync with her emotions. She was fine, wasn't she? It had gone well. She had survived. Tears streamed down her cheeks. Sobs heaved themselves out of her chest. Sorry, she said. I'm not sure what's happening to me.

It's okay, Camille said. It's to be expected.

It is?

Of course! I've done this a few times now, and this happens every time.

Were the directors there? In the audience?

Oh yes, Camille said. They were both there, in among the paying audience.

That was… a real show?

Listen, Zara. This is how Intimacy works. We utilize your genuine emotion, your vulnerability and, well, your fear, I suppose. It has a real potent energy, the kind that can't be faked. You were fantastic tonight. James had a lot of fun playing off you, I could tell.

I thought there would be rehearsals.

Nope, no rehearsals for you. That's just an added bonus, Camille said with a wink. I suppose the audition was a rehearsal of sorts. I was watching you at the time, in a different room, via streaming. What a great audition that was! You were so up for it, up for anything. I loved the Kylie Minogue, too. A stroke of genius.

Oh. Well. Thank you, Zara stammered. She hadn't realized the audition was being filmed.

Listen. There's a car downstairs waiting to take you home. I'm sure you need a minute to catch your breath. Or, if you need to, you can go through to the next office, where our mental health team are waiting. They can debrief you, help you check in with your feelings, that sort of thing.

When Zara spoke, her voice sounded as though it was coming from somewhere else, a few metres away. I think I just want to go home, she said.

The next morning, Zara woke early. She watched the morning light seep through the cracks in her curtains, slowly, slowly, until the room was blasted with sunshine. She felt raw and empty, like she'd been scraped out. Candice phoned, but she didn't answer. She listened to the voice message: *I was in the front row. You were simply incredible!* There was a text message from her mum, too. She deleted it, unread.

It had been a rough initiation, but Zara decided she would go back. She would ask for another shot. In fact, she was looking forward to it. She understood what was expected of her this time. In her notebook, she mapped out the beats of the performance – when James's character tipped from anger to despair, and how her character had responded to that sudden emotional shift. Even though she'd felt wrung out and depleted after the performance, on balance, she decided that *Intimacy* was incredibly innovative. They took risks, and she liked that. It was a truly exciting concept, one she was thrilled to be part of. She decided to bring along some of her favourite affirmation cards to read before she went onstage: *I choose an amazing life. I accept all of my uniqueness and quirks. I forgive myself and learn from my mistakes. I am in control of how I feel, and today I choose happiness.*

When she arrived at the theatre that afternoon, Albert seemed surprised to see her.

Back so soon? he said.

Zara laughed. Of course!

She moved to head upstairs, but Albert stopped her.

Let me call Camille, he said.

Camille arrived in moments. She was brisk but unruffled, her usual self. She led Zara up to the same office from the day before, with its rows of ominously silent computers, their blank screens. Out of the window, there was no view. Only a crack of blue sky and a brick wall. Camille tapped away on a laptop, her faced fixed in concentration.

Zara cleared her throat. I have some ideas, she said. For tonight?

Camille nodded but did not move her eyes from the screen.

Time passed. Every so often, Zara heard voices and commotion from behind the door. She readied herself each time, took deep breaths and arranged her face and body just so, but no one ever came in. She checked the time on her phone, once, twice. It was nearly seven o'clock. Camille was still typing. Every so often she switched between her laptop and her phone, clicking away in a never-ending stream.

Um, Camille?

Camille nodded.

Should I... get ready?

Camille blinked. Ready for what?

For the performance tonight.

Oh. Camille blinked again and rubbed her forehead. Right. Listen, Zara...

There were voices coming from outside the door. Zara stood up and moved towards it. Through the square window, she could see someone who looked like Camille – dressed all in black, wearing a headset, hair scraped back – talking to a young woman.

It's all right, not-Camille said. Trust me, it's you they're waiting for.

But I... I can't do it. I need to prepare... I have a process. I thought I was here for an audition. A recall.

Not-Camille shifted her body slightly to the side and Zara saw that the young woman she was talking to was Casey Day.

What's Casey doing here? she said softly.

Camille placed a hand on the door and muttered something into her radio. Zara thought she heard the words 'mental health first-aiders', but she couldn't be sure. She watched Casey through the window. Her face was contorted with anguish, washed in the blue backstage lighting. Her eyes threatened tears. But she still looked beautiful.

Listen to me, Zara, Camille said, her hand still putting pressure on the door as though she thought Zara would push through and try to escape. Remember I told you yesterday about how *Intimacy* works?

Zara imagined herself pushing Camille out of the way and running through the door, past Casey and not-Camille and onto the stage, where the audience, the lights were waiting. It would be easy. It should be easy.

Intimacy is about real feelings, Camille continued. Deep feelings. The ones that surprise you, the ones that can't be scripted. The ones you don't even understand yourself. And do you remember what else I said?

Zara said nothing. She watched not-Camille take Casey firmly by the arm and lead her towards the door with the sign above it that read PERFORMANCE IN PROGRESS.

Intimacy thrives on something that cannot be faked, Camille said. You can't do it again. It's done. Over.

A man and a woman in matching blue T-shirts walked down the corridor towards the office. They didn't rush. Emblazoned on their chests, the words MENTAL HEALTH.

But I want to, Zara said. I want to do it again. She could hear blood in her ears, its sickening wet thump. She should open the door. This was her last shot. Now, she told herself, but her body remained where it was, pressed up against the door. She couldn't feel it any more. It wasn't hers to control.

You can't, Camille said firmly but not unkindly. This time you will know what's coming. You will be acting, and that isn't what we want.

Casey had disappeared by now, gone to take her next shot at fame and immortality. Not-Camille was back in the corridor, speaking into her radio, though Zara could hardly see her around the bodies of the two mental health people. They were coming closer and closer, their warm, friendly faces filling up the window. One of them knocked softly on the office door.

Everything's going to be all right, Zara, one of them said, their voice muffled behind the glass.

But I can do it better, Zara said, turning to Camille one last time. Please. Just give me another chance. Let me try again.

ACKNOWLEDGEMENTS

I wouldn't have finished writing this book without the guidance, encouragement and feedback of many, many brilliant people. I am so fortunate to know you all.

Thank you to Julia Bell, Abi Curtis, Alison Winch and Naomi Wood for feedback on this project in its PhD iteration. I will be forever thankful for Jean McNeil and Karen Schaller, my supervisory dream team, who have taught me so much about writing and life.

Thank you to Mick Nolan for publishing my first story in *The Tangerine* and for encouraging me to take my time in a world that always wants to rush us. Thank you to Ben Pester for generous and incredibly helpful feedback on one of these stories.

I am grateful to Melissa Febos for generously allowing her words to be used as an epigraph to this collection. Her writing, especially in the book *Girlhood*, has blown open doors in my mind. Thank you.

A very big thank you to everyone who has worked on this book. Special thanks to my wonderful agent Sara Langham at DHA for guiding me through this whole process with such poise and kindness, and to my brilliant editor, Susie Nicklin, for being so enthusiastic every step of the way.

Thank you to my family: Zoe, Tamsin, Janet, Mark, Helen, Megan and Nia. And, of course, thank you to Ruby, Sonny, Theo, Hazel, Ardie and Caelan for being such rays of sunshine. Thank you to my friends: in particular Tori, Sarah, Jess, Danielle and Stacey. Most of all, thank you to Isabella, Idris and Owen for making every day of my life so special – I love you and you are amazing.

Transforming a manuscript into the book you hold in your hands is a group project.

Marni would like to thank everyone who helped to publish *I HOPE YOU'RE HAPPY*.

THE INDIGO PRESS TEAM
Susie Nicklin
Phoebe Barker
Michelle O'Neill
Will Atkinson

JACKET DESIGN
Luke Bird

PUBLICITY
Sophie Portas

EDITORIAL PRODUCTION
Tetragon

COPY-EDITOR
Sarah Terry

PROOFREADER
Madeleine Rogers

THE
INDIGO
PRESS

The Indigo Press is an independent publisher of contemporary fiction and non-fiction, based in London. Guided by a spirit of internationalism, feminism and social justice, we publish books to make readers see the world afresh, question their behaviour and beliefs, and imagine a better future.

Browse our books and sign up to our newsletter for special offers and discounts:

theindigopress.com

Follow *The Indigo Press* on social media for the latest news, events and more:

ⓧ @PressIndigoThe
ⓞ @TheIndigoPress
ⓕ @TheIndigoPress
ⓞ The Indigo Press
ⓙ @theindigopress